Navicular Syndrome

Books by Jaime Jackson

Equine
The Natural Horse: Lessons from the Wild (1992, rev. 2020)
Horse Owners Guide to Natural Hoof Care (1999, rev. 2002)
Founder – Prevention and Cure the Natural Way (2001)
Guide To Booting Horses for Hoof Care Professionals (2002)
Paddock Paradise: A Guide to Natural Horse Boarding (2005, rev. 2018)
The Natural Trim: Principles and Practice (2012, rev. 2019)
The Healing Angle: Nature's Gateway to the Healing Field (2014)
Laminitis: An Equine Plague of Unconscionable Proportions (2016)
Training Manual: ISNHCP Natural Trim Training Program (2017)
the Hoof Balancer: A Unique Tool for Balancing Equine Hooves (2019)
The Natural Trim: Basic Guidelines (2019)
The Natural Trim: Advanced Guidelines (2019)
Navicular Syndrome: Healing And Prevention Using the Principles and Practices of Natural Horse Care (2021)

Other
Guard Your Teeth: Why the Dental Industry Fails Us – A Guide to Natural Dental Care (2018)
Buckskin Tanner: A Guide to Natural Hide Tanning (2019)
Cheyenne Tipi Notes: Technical Insights Into 19th Century Plains Indian Bison Hide Tanning (2019)
Living Behind the Facade: Memoirs Of A Gay Man's Journey Through the 20th Century (2019) George Somers with Jaime Jackson
Platform: A Humanitarian Model For An Egalitarian Society (2019)
Zoo Paradise: A New Model for Humane Zoological Gardens (2019)

Forthcoming
Horse Trek – Into the Mystic

Navicular Syndrome

Healing and Prevention
Using the Principles and Practices
of Natural Horse Care
Based On the U.S. Great Basin
Wild Horse Model

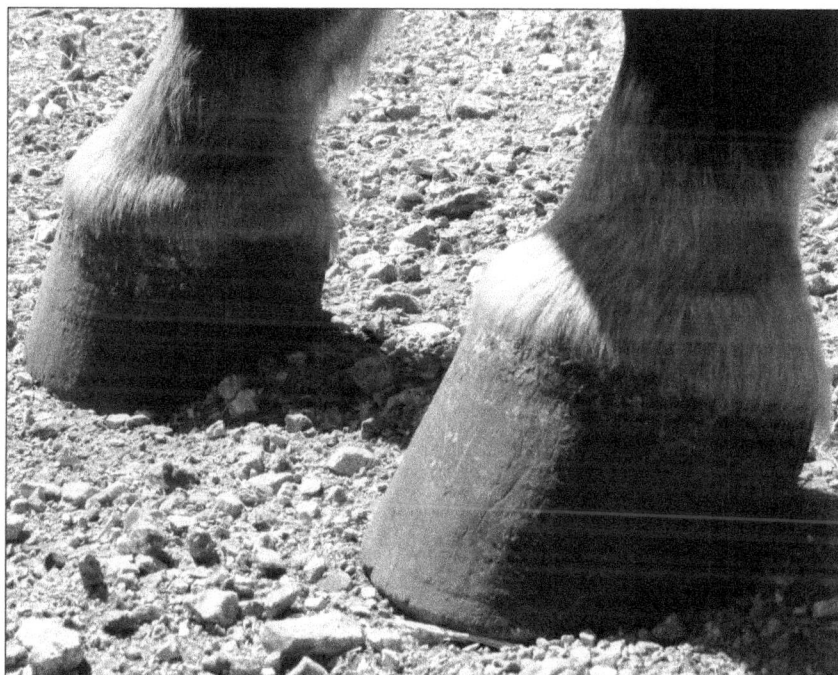

Jaime Jackson
Author, *The Natural Horse:
Lessons From the Wild*

J. JACKSON PUBLISHING

J. Jackson Publishing
P.O. Box 1765
Harrison, AR 72601
info@isnhcp.net

ISBN: 978-1-7355358-1-4

Manufactured in the United States of America by
Ingram Book Company (https://www.ingramcontent.com)

Neither the author, contributors nor J. Jackson Publishing will accept responsibility for any illness, injury, or death resulting from your use and/or application of this work. The ideas, procedures, and suggestions contained in this book are not meant as substitutes for consultation with your own veterinarian, hoof care provider, or other professional. You, the reader, are strongly urged to use your own judgment, intuition, and common sense in utilizing this book.

Contents

Trimming Audrey's right front clubfoot. See Chapter 5 for details.

Preface

My first awareness of what is known today as navicular syndrome or navicular disease, or simply *navicular* — as I will call it throughout this book — dates back to the 1970s when I was a novice farrier. Navicular expresses itself in two ways: the horse faltering very noticeably, favoring one or the other of the front limbs *but not both*; and by what is called *clubfoot*, a distinct change in just one of the front hooves. The clubfoot is referred to as such due to its conspicuously upright (steep angle of growth) and contracted appearance. Or so when contrasted with the other front hoof that appears larger (e.g., wider) and lower angled. Logically, the clubfoot is then believed to be a pathological corruption of the hoof, and, therefore, the source of the horse's lameness. But how did this condition of a limping horse with a clubfoot come to be called "navicular?"

Today, as it was back then, navicular is thought to be an inflammation of the navicular bone (from which navicular gets its name), its bursa (a small serous sac between a tendon and a bone), and the (deep digital) flexor tendon that naturally moves against the bone and bursa to flex the hoof. Excessive pressure and friction by the tendon purportedly causes the erosional damage, and, thus, the pain and limping. Worse, the condition never seems to heal. And for this reason, navicular horses, no longer able to serve their purpose as "beasts of burden," are commonly put down. "Who wants to own or invest in a permanently damaged horse?" I've heard more than once in the horse-using community. But I've also witnessed navicular horses sold and resold "down the line" to unwitting horse owners who simply didn't know better. Such unscrupulous behavior eventually ends when someone finally takes the horse to a sale barn, thence to an abattoir. I've investigated the entire path of navicular from soundness to the fatal ending.

Historically, farriers and vets have always struggled to help such horses. This is reflected in their textbooks and professional magazines that deal with equine lameness. I suspect navicular has been a lameness issue since the days of the specie's domestication 5,000 or more years ago. But current thinking is that navicular has no cure, and so it really comes down to treating signs and symptoms, real or imagined, to bring as much comfort as possible to the horse, short of euthanasia if possible. This was my thinking, too, back then.

At that time, professional farriers considered that the cause of navicular might very well be due to the horse's genetics (e.g., the breed). Or how the hooves are trimmed or shod, or both. I recall considerable discussion about what to do, accompanied by much experimentation. For example, it was thought that by raising or lowering the tilt or angle of the hoof through various shoeing procedures, tendon pressure upon the bone could be mitigated and, thus, bring relief to the horse, and, hopefully, facilitate a healing. Vets even joined in, thinking that surgical scoring of the tendon to lessen tension, or even a neurectomy to desensitize the entire foot, might help. But nothing seemed to work, and few could agree on anything. New to the profession, I observed and listened carefully, but held my tongue. I was as confounded as anyone.

One day in late 1977, a client of mine gave me a newly published book that focused on the problem of navicular.* The authors believed that shortening the toe wall and elevating the heels (by various mechanical means), such that the angles of the front and hind toe walls came into alignment with the angles of the shoulder and hip joints respectively, was the direction farriers should pursue. This alignment, they proposed, was what was natural for the equine species. Many attempts by many different farriers around the world tried the new method. But, as with other methods, this one also failed. But in their text, the authors pointed directly to wild horses in their native states as a basis for their logic. This statement brought me into contact, and eventually, a professional relationship, with the principal author, Leslie Emery, and, several years later, face-to-face with America's wild, free-roaming horses.*

Over a four year period beginning in the early 1980s, I traveled among different bands of these wild horses that were inhabiting the vast, unfenced rangelands of the U.S. Great Basin. Eventually, my investigations led me into the wild horse processing corrals of the U.S. Bureau of Land Management (BLM), where these horses were transitioned from lives in the wild, to lives in captivity. At the corrals, I measured a thousand or more of their hooves. As in their home ranges, never once did I observe a single lame horse with a clubfoot — in other words, navicular.* In short order, I came to believe, as I do to this day, that navicular (with lameness) has no matrix in the horse's foot, but in "the minds of men." And that the lameness is actually due to trauma of the upper body, and that it is almost entirely man-made. I have since then also come to the opinion that navicular is preventable. And, under certain conditions that I will discuss later, healable such that the horse is no longer lame.

But there is much to sort through if one is to come to an understanding of the entire basis of navicular. Perhaps the foremost obstacle

*Horseshoeing Theory and Hoof Care. Emery, Miller, and Van Hoosen. (1977, Lea & Febiger).

*But there is much more to the story that brought me into wild horse country than this book. That is the subject of my autobiographical account in a new book I am currently working on, *Horse Trek: Into the Mystic*.

*Corroborated by Dr. Ric Redden. *The Wild Horse's Foot*. 2001 - 14th Annual Bluegrass Laminitis Symposium Notes. Written and presented January 2001 by R.F. (Ric) Redden, DVM.

to this end is the name itself. It is misleading, a misnomer actually, and that alone has condemned countless navicular horses to lives of misery and early death. Worse, as a corridor of misunderstanding to unwitting horse owners, it pre-condemns many more horses to the worst navicular outcomes. This is a dilemma I have wrestled with for decades, and will undoubtedly continue to do so for many more years. "Is there," I've asked myself countless times, "a starting point from which to change the discussion away from navicular nomenclature and mythology to the facts of the matter?" As it turns out, there is a parallel example in equine pathology: laminitis.

Like "navicular disease," there is also "laminitis disease," colloquially referred to as "laminitis." But laminitis is no more a disease of the horse's foot than is navicular. Yet both have become "barnyard words" with precisely that understanding across the horse-using community in every equestrian discipline. Personally, I found my way out of this conundrum by simply recognizing laminitis for what it truly is: an inflammatory *response* to a disease.* This book will track along the same lines as laminitis, my attempt to bring the facts of navicular into full view for what it is — also a symptom of a much bigger problem. One the horse using community must bring itself to face and correct. As with laminitis, it is both necessary and the right thing to do.

*"Whole Horse Inflammatory Disease (WHID)." *Laminitis: A Plague of Unconscionable Proportions.* (2016) Jaime Jackson.

The Wild Horse Model

I n arriving at this book, you have entered onto one of several path-ways leading into what is called the "wild horse model." This model is based on the lifestyles of America's wild, free-roaming horses living in the U.S. Great Basin. What it teaches us, in the most fundamental of ways, is what a horse is. Not what we may think a horse is or should be, but what natural selection has created over a million years ago through the evolutionary descent of the equine species, *Equus ferus ferus.**

My first attempt to bring this model to domesticated horses oc-curred in my book, *The Natural Horse: Lessons From the Wild.*** A door opener to the model, I eventually penned other books delving further into the nuances of the horse's natural state. As always, I did this for the singular purpose of helping horses living in captivity among hu-mans. As segues from the wild horse model to the "whole horse" con-cept of natural horse care (NHC), I grouped these "lessons from the wild" into four categories. These are known as the 4 Pillars of NHC: (1) natural boarding (Paddock Paradise), (2) a reasonably natural diet, (3) natural horsemanship, and (4) the natural trim. This book explores the potential healing forces of these Pillars as they relate to navicular.

Navicular, according to this book's thesis, has its origins principally in extreme riding and training practices that permanently break down some part of the musculoskelature of the horse. This trauma results in lameness and club foot; hence, the 3rd Pillar of natural horsemanship is an important discussion relative to the prevention of navicular.

Although relatively rare compared to egregiously harmful eques-trian practices, navicular may also result if the horse's boarding condi-tions are unsafe and conducive to serious body injuries. Here, the 1st Pillar, natural boarding, or more specifically, Paddock Paradise,* cannot be exempted from the discussion as it can both prevent such outcomes and provide a healing pathway for navicular in its own right. Paddock Paradise is a tracking system serving as a 24/7 living space for horses. The equine species is an animal of prey, and, like all prey species, the freedom to move ("fight or flight response*") at liberty at all times is critical to their mental and physical health — and vitality.

Other factors may also be causal or contributing to the horse's lame-ness, but which have nothing to do with navicular. Diets that trigger

E. ferus ferus is the ancient antece-dent of the modern horse, *E. cabal-lus*. The same species, they are ge-netically indistinguishable from each other.

***The Natural Horse: Lessons From the Wild*. Jaime Jackson. (1992, North-land Publishing; rev. 2020)

Paddock Paradise: A Guide to Natural Horse Boarding. Jaime Jackson. (1995, rev. 2018)

*Also called "acute stress response."

4

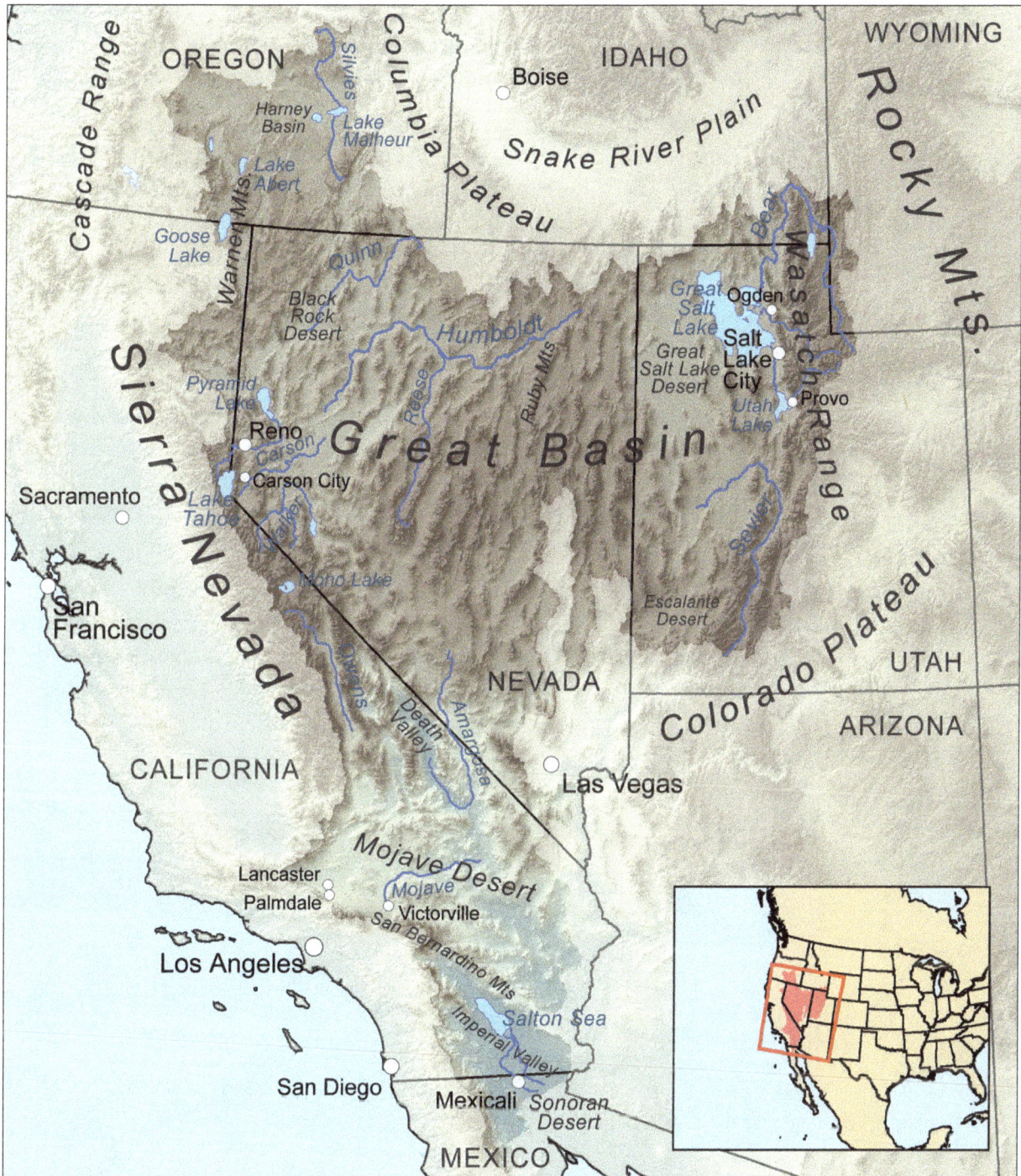

The U.S. Great Basin, home to America's wild, free-roaming horses, our model for natural hoof care.

Laminitis: A Plague of Unconscionable Proportions. (2016) Jaime Jackson.

laminitis are most common.* In fact, navicular and laminitis are typically so intertwined that to confirm a diagnosis of navicular, the effects of laminitis must first be resolved. This necessitates introducing the 2nd Pillar (a reasonably natural diet) and the effects of "slipper toe" (4th Pillar, the natural trim) if we are to confirm navicular at all.

The Natural Trim: Basic Guidelines. Jaime Jackson. (2019)

Looking to the hooves (4th Pillar), the supreme importance of the natural trim is also discussed.* At the core of the natural trim is what I call the Theory of H°. H° ("Healing Angle") refers specifically to the growth behavior of the hoof in captivity, in contrast to N°, its counterpart in the wild equine state. Like N° (from which H° is statistically derived), H° is also a specific measurement. Simply stated, measurable changes in H° towards N° inure to greater soundness, while changes away from N° are normally cause for concern. An exception would be the migrational behavior of H° away from N° towards the clubfoot conformation. Here, H°'s behavior provides important information about what is happening to the horse due to navicular. Thus, although very technical in its application, the Theory of H° is a critical tool in the diagnosis, prevention and, in certain instances, healing of navicular.

It is my hope that this book, in the broadest way possible through all 4 Pillars of NHC, will serve the horse owner in preventing navicular in their horses in the first place. Or, if the horse is already diagnosed with it, then to mitigate its effects while hoping for a restoration to soundness.

What Causes Navicular?

Every horse has its physical and mental limits when it comes to how they are ridden or trained. When such practices are taken to extremes, and repeatedly so, the likely outcome is permanent damage to the horse's body, accompanied by debilitating pain, faltering (limping) over one front leg, and clubfoot. Which is to say, navicular. Three questions immediately arise: Where exactly does the body break down, resulting in navicular? Why does this breakdown result in faltering in one front limb only? And why does the clubfoot occur if there is no pathological corruption of the hoof?

As I began to formulate the concept of NHC (natural horse care) based on the wild horse model as a way of interpreting problems plaguing horses, it was only logical that I would look not just at the horse's hooves, or even the entire body, but to all 4 Pillars. This strategy was extremely important in elucidating navicular causality, just as it was in understanding laminitis pathogenesis.* Had I remained "stuck at the hoof," for example, like others in my profession, the bigger picture could never have come into focus. Indeed, farriers — and even barefooters who do not embrace the wild horse model — are so locked into targeting the hoof as the problem, that the mere suggestion that the clubfoot is not the problem, and "worse," that it should be left alone, would make no sense at all. Such thinking was, and still is, heretical, and grounds for my leaving the profession. The final straw came when I pointed not at the clubfoot, but to the rider on the horse as the culprit. My days as a farrier serving horse owners were then over. One cannot blame the hand that feeds you. I then made a conscious and vocal decision to serve the horse, terminating my professional relationship to the industry as a farrier in a single letter sent to every client when I began writing The Natural Horse in the late 1980s. Horses would hence go barefoot under the guidance of the wild horse model, or my services would no longer be available. Most declined, and one might argue, that letter signaled the beginning of the NHC revolution.

*Pathogenesis is the origination and development of a disease.

It is interesting that all the upper body (that is, anywhere above the hoof) problems associated with clubfoot were there all along. I just couldn't make the connection to navicular until the wild horse model opened the doors of NHC so that I could see them for what they were. Still, it was hard for me to say to an owner, you or your trainer are destroying your horse by the way your are training or riding them. Yet, it was true. But this was the 1980s and NHC as it is widely known today, did not exist yet. Horse owners with navicular horses listened to their vets and farriers, not to a renegade trimmer like myself pointing to a "wild horse model" that no one had ever heard of! And worse, how do you prove anything to someone not wanting to hear what you have to say? Well, the fact is, you can't.

Even with the wild horse model, the connections between the point of body damage, the single faltering limb, and the mysterious clubfoot had to be figured out. To be honest, at first none of it made any sense to me. For example, why would damage to a left hind limb cause the horse to falter on the right front limb? Moreover, why would a horse seemingly falter at the trot, but not in the other gaits? Until I had this much figured out, the enigma of the clubfoot would remain just that.

§

The idea that the trot was revealing of faltering, and that the clubfoot had a possible relationship to it, brought me to thinking about the horse's left and right leads. "What if," I asked myself, "a horse favored a particular lead, but wasn't able to take the opposite lead equally for whatever reason?" This triggered a memory from my readings of Alois Podhajsky's observations of leads possibly being influenced by what he called "crookedness."* Podhajsky warned that crookedness in horses was a "fault" that had to be corrected during training if the horse is to be balanced under the rider and able to "collect" themselves naturally in the higher levels of dressage. He called this "straightening" so that the horse may take either their left or right lead while fully balanced and naturally collected with "rounded" backs that are able to carry the rider's weight without damaging the spine (Figures 1-1 and 1-2). According to Podhajsky:

> A horse may not accept the bit evenly on both sides. He will make himself stiff on one side and will follow the slightest action of the rein on the other by turning his head. He will take a firmer contact and only reluctantly follow the action of the rein on the side on which he is stiff. On the other side he will anticipate the action of the rein and bend this way; this to say, he becomes hollow on this side. When the reins are applied evenly the horse will bend his neck to the hollow side, on which he will not accept the rein. The rider will be able to recognize this as the rein will not touch the neck on this hollow side, whereas it lies close to the neck on the side on which the horse makes himself stiff.*

An explanation for this, in my opinion, is that from birth the muscles of the horse are naturally more compressed on one side of their body than the other; meaning, they have a "short" or concaved side, and a complementary "long" or convex side. The term "crooked" is derived

*Alois Podhajsky, *The Complete Training Of Horse and Rider* (Doubleday/1966). Colonel Podhajsky commanded the Spanish Riding School's training of horses and riders. He was a Silver Medallist in the dressage competition at the 1936 Olympics in Berlin, Germany.

*Podhajsky, *The Complete Training Of Horse and Rider*. P. 43.

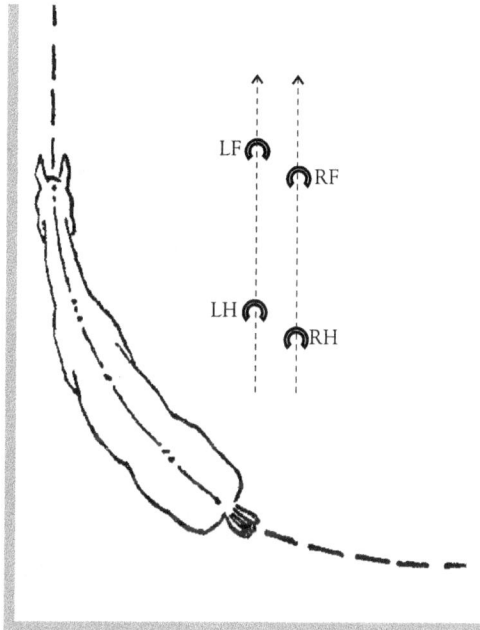

Figure 1-1: Straightness

The horse bends evenly through the body in the arc of the turn. In this case, he is moving to the right, but he is equally able to bend to the left and sustain the same arc of motion. Such a horse assumes rein contact equally on both sides, according to Podhajsky. He is said to be "straight" in that he has no "hollow" and "stiff" sides, and is physically able to track forward bending to one side or the other. Both sides are equally strong and able to carry the weight of the rider in the extended and accelerated paces. Moving straight forward, his hooves form two trails of hoof tracks as seen in the illustration.

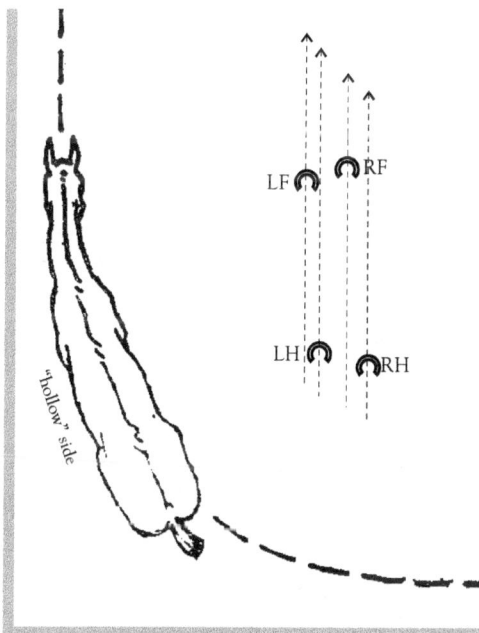

Figure 1-2: Crookedness

The horse is unable to bend evenly through the body to his right. The side against the wall is his hollow side. He would bend readily in that direction but would be unable to accept rein contact. Such a horse is said to be "crooked," resulting in multi-tracks when moving straight forward. If not straightened through systemized gymnastic exercises or a natural lifestyle, he is at extreme risk of becoming navicular and possibly irreparably lame.

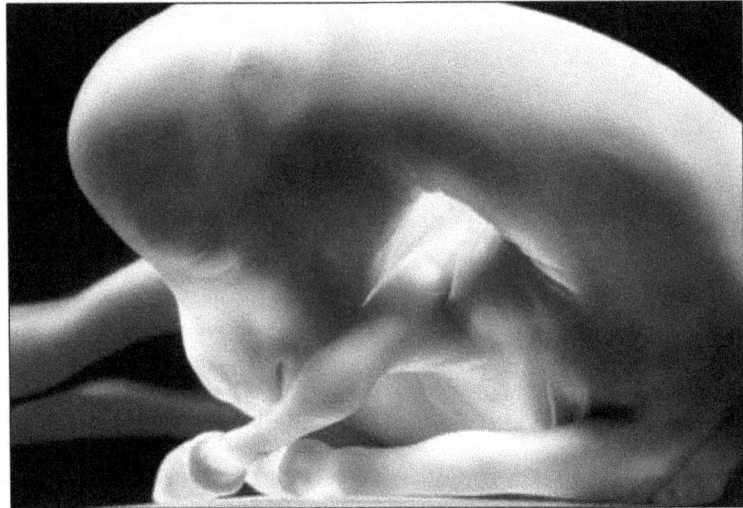

Figure 1-3. *En utero* position of the horse has not been overlooked by some of the great equestrians of the past, including Podhajsky. *The Complete Training Of Horse and Rider.* P. 46.

from this difference. There is some suggestion that crookedness could follow from the predisposition of the developing fetus in the womb, where it is typically "bent" to one side for months on end (Figure *1-3*).

Without straightening, crooked horses ridden beyond the most basic, free forward movements (e.g., casual trail riding) could cause them great harm. Podhajsky, pointing directly at navicular, warns again:

> The correct bend of the hind legs must be brought about by all three joints being bent equally and to the same degree. If the hocks only are bent, as is often the case [in poorly trained horses], the bend will be of little value and the horse will be prematurely worn out as in all likelihood it will lead to spavins or thoroughpins.*

Podhajsky's and others similar observations made sense to me, particularly as it applied to my own thesis that extreme riding practices cause navicular. I then reasoned that navicular could arise from both crooked horses and horses simply forced to move beyond their natural limits, crooked or straight. But, additionally, I also recalled my own hoof measurement data gathered at the BLM corrals, which showed that horses did not fully mature, including their musculoskelature, until five or more years following birth (Figure 1-4).** In fact, years before I entered wild horse country, I was fully aware as a farrier that horses ridden before maturity not only caused harm, but could cripple them for life, if they weren't sent off to the sale barn instead.

Podhajsky's insights were also helpful in answering why faltering occurs not only at the trot over the front limb, but also "diagonally" across the horse's body. While he has shown why natural collection is not possible with a crooked horse in any of the natural gaits, it is at the trot, particularly during a turn, that faltering due to navicular is most pronounced. For example, let us assume that a horse is crooked and, further, there is damage to their lumbar spine or rear legs. To begin

*Podhajsky, *Training of Horse and Rider,* p. 51. *Spavin* is calcified or bony enlargement of the hock due to excessive strain. *Thoroughpin is* synovial swelling above the hock on both sides of the hind leg. Both spavin and thoroughpin are associated with lameness caused by unnatural riding practices that compel the horse to move excessively outside the limits of their natural gaits. — JJ

**The Natural Horse.* p. 71.

Figure 1-4: Impact of Age on Hoof Size

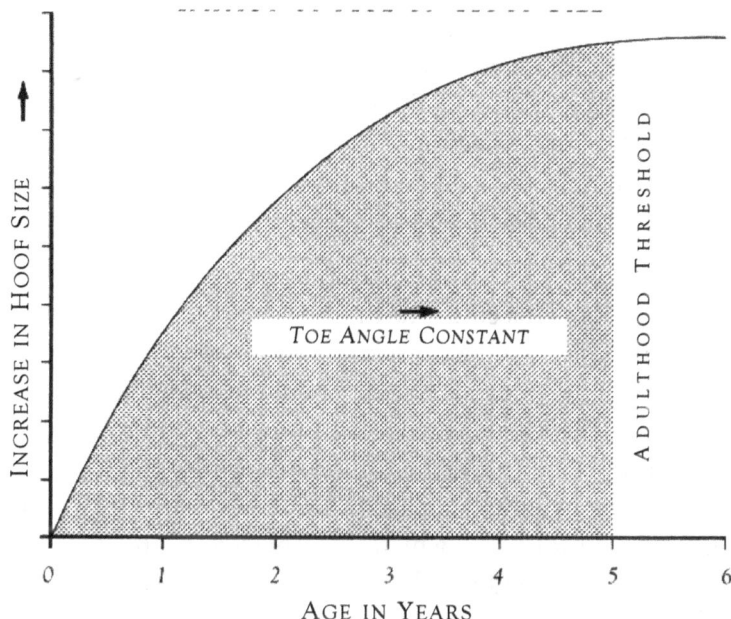

INCREASE IN HOOF SIZE

TOE ANGLE CONSTANT

ADULTHOOD THRESHOLD

0   1   2   3   4   5   6

AGE IN YEARS

with, the hind limbs cannot naturally collect to support more body weight and also provide thrust for forward movement due to crookedness. On top of this, in this scenario, there is severe body damage (spine or hind legs). Accordingly, one or the other front limb must somehow take up the slack (carry the load or weight-bearing force) of the doubly compromised hind limb — or the horse will simply collapse. This compensatory action results in the faltering upon the "over-loaded" front limb. The more severe the damage to the body, the more pronounced is the faltering. To aid in the transfer of weight from the hindquarters to the forelimb that is taking up the slack, nature transforms the hoof of that forelimb into the upright clubfoot conformation. In this interpretation, the clubfoot is acting analogously as a modified "crutch" a human would use (Figure 1-5).

I believe the clubfoot response to upper body injury is a specialized adaptation, similar to the horse's winter coat providing protection in winter, waning in spring, and then disappearing come summer. In the wild, to the extent that clubfoot may happen, it would be a more transitory transformation — it can come and go, like the winter coat — to compensate for less than permanent body damage. I believe this is a possibility, although there is no direct evidence of it happening in Great Basin wild, free-roaming horses. Extreme permanent

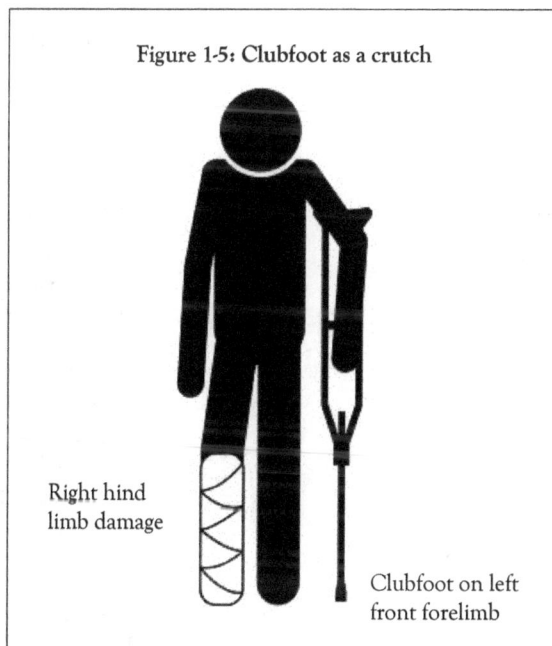

Figure 1-5: Clubfoot as a crutch

Right hind limb damage

Clubfoot on left front forelimb

11

damage resulting in pain and gait obstruction (i.e., lameness) would have attracted predators in the evolution of the horse, leading to the animal's immediate death. The clubfoot would then have had little survival value. However, few injuries in the wild appear to be life-threatening, and so clubfoot in the pre-navicular sense would be logical in the stream of natural selection. For this reason, "transitional club-foot" would be rare in the wild and sampling of hooves would have to be expanded considerably to witness and confirm it.

But on this point another distinction must be made regarding faltering and clubfoot. This concerns injuries due to dangerous boarding conditions. I trimmed such a horse that was impaled by a stake-like object left in the animal's corral. It had penetrated a shoulder muscle causing great internal tissue damage. Faltering and clubfoot followed. I have also followed veterinary surgical intrusions into the foot to treat clubfoot, resulting in actual damage to the "navicular zone." Severe faltering and clubfoot followed, which never healed. In these types of cases, we are no longer talking about horsemanship-based navicular, but simply irreversible damage caused by an object left in the horse's living quarters or equally damaging surgery done to the horse's foot.

Common areas of body damage leading to equestrian navicular

On the facing page I have identified areas of the horse's body that are commonly damaged by equestrian practices leading to navicular (Figure 1-6). While these reflect skeletal and joint traumas, they can be traced to crookedness, inadequate muscular development, excessive or repetitive use of a body part, and biological immaturity.

Foremost is the lumbar region of the spine anywhere between the thoracic and pelvic vertebrae. Running one's hand along the lumbar spine of a navicular horse with "lower back" damage will reveal hard lumps. The rider is literally breaking the horse's back, and nature's healing response is to "weld" the area shut to prevent further damage (Figure (1-7) There is some evidence of this occurring also in the cervical spine where forced "head carriage" breaks the horse's neck. But x-rays or other high technology would be needed to confirm this.

Damage to the hocks, fetlocks, and knees are also common. And I have seen any of these along with damaged spines on the same horse. In fact, any hard swelling of tissue associated with these joints along with nearby tendons is cause to believe the horse is navicular. I have not seen signs of navicular in cases of "bowed tendons" in the front legs, only because the horses I've witnessed it happening to were simply euthanized straight away to put them out of their misery. It goes without saying, the clubfoot would have had no time to develop anyway.

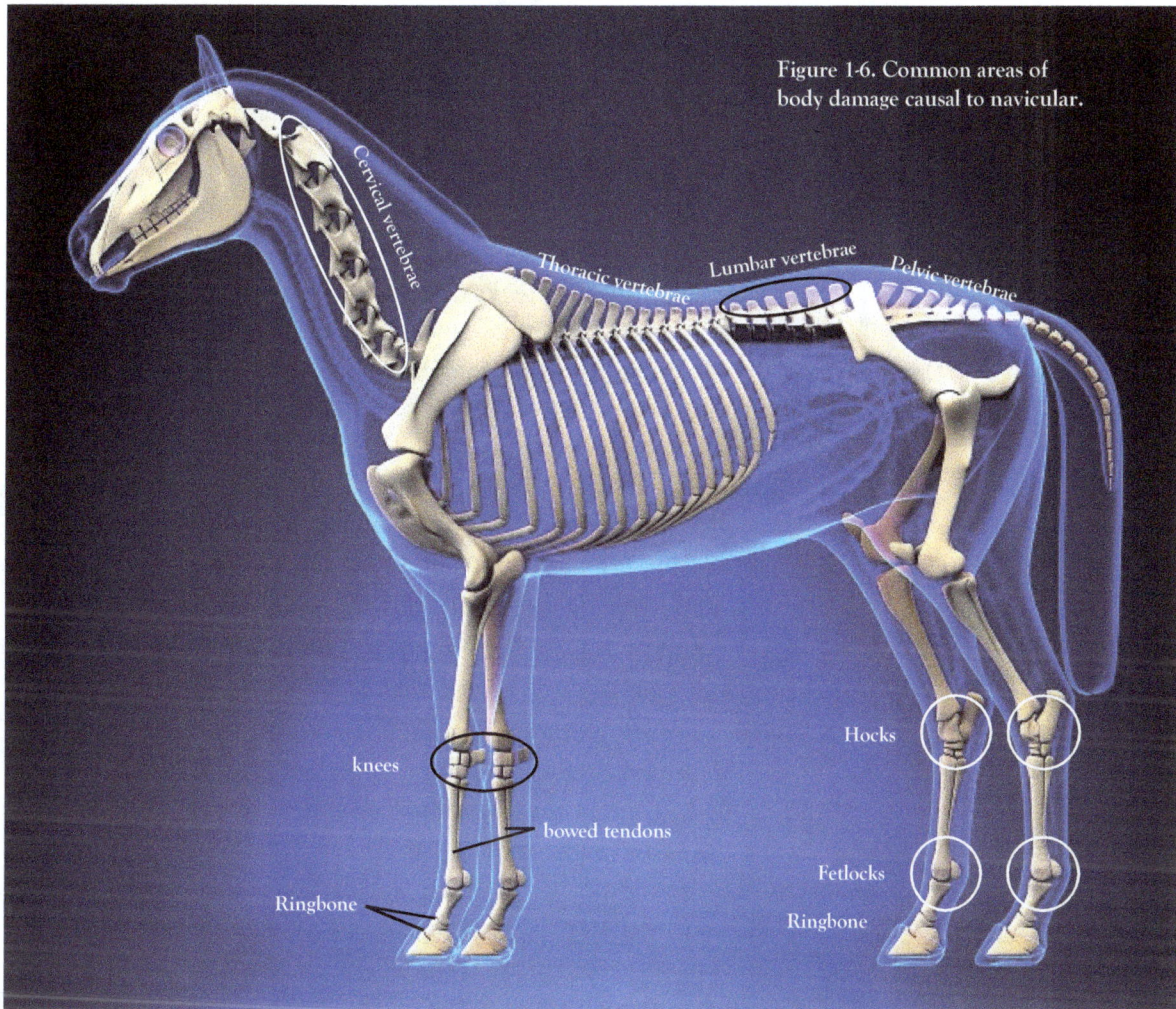

Figure 1-6. Common areas of body damage causal to navicular.

Cervical vertebrae

Thoracic vertebrae

Lumbar vertebrae

Pelvic vertebrae

knees

Hocks

bowed tendons

Fetlocks

Ringbone

Ringbone

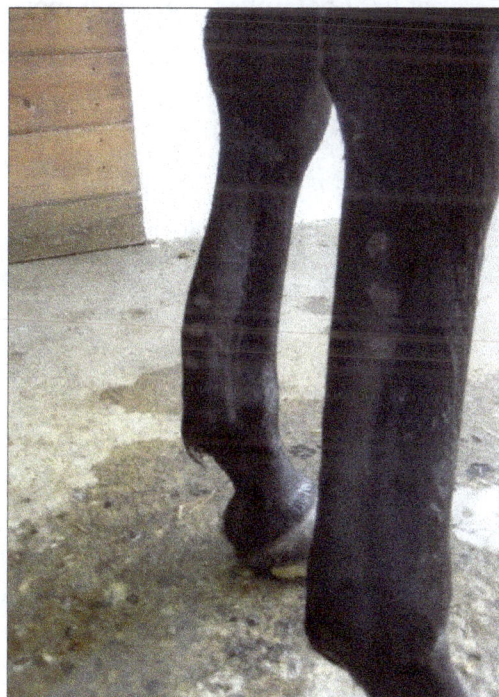

Figure 1-7. The impact of navicular is not unlike ringbone of the pastern and coffin joints (*left*), and (bilateral) bowed tendons (*right*). Both are catastrophic outcomes of extreme horsemanship practices that permanently lame the horse.

CHAPTER TWO
NHC Pillar #1
Paddock Paradise: A Healing Field

If unnatural locomotion breaks down the horse, leaving them lame and in pain, Paddock Paradise is what can restore their vitality better than any other equine confinement system. This is because Paddock Paradise facilitates natural equine behavior, which favors the natural gaits on the animal's own terms. The tracking and pathing network of Paddock Paradise mimics the natural pathways wild horses (and other wild quadrupeds*) create for themselves in their open rangelands. Such freedom to move naturally favors restoration of damaged bodies, including the hooves if they also have been harmed.

*See my book, *Zoo Paradise*.

In March of 2013, "Audrey," a 14 year old Arabian mare (*below*), entered the Paddock Paradise at the AANHCP field headquarters near the village of Lompoc along the central coast of California (USA). Audrey had developed the classic clubfoot following training as a four year old in the reining horse discipline. At this point, training ended and she became, first, a brood mare, and later a pleasure (light trail/arena) riding horse. At some point in her history, she became chronically laminitic, arriving that way at our facility. Audrey's hooves revealed a cascade of stress rings (Figures 2-1 thru 2-3), indicating that the effects of chronic laminitis were still in play. The bearing surfaces of her hoof walls were also chipped and split, typical of unnatural hoof care and laminitic hooves. Remarkably, H° was readable on the HMR.

(*Below*) Audrey, wearing a clubfoot and laminitic, living the "stall life" before arriving in our Paddock Paradise. (*Right*) Audrey not long after being turned out "on track." Our Paddock Paradise simulates the wilderness habitat of Great Basin wild, free-roaming horses. Horses instinctively feel at home in such a habitat. Although there was a long stretch of unfenced track in our upper pasture, not once did they use it to "escape."

(Figure 2-1) *Black arrow* points to numerous stress rings circumscribing the entirety of Audrey's brittle right front (clubbed) hoof, from the hairline down to ground level. *White arrow* points to quarter crack, also running from the hairline down to ground level. *Yellow arrow* points to a missing layer of outer wall stripped from the hoof.

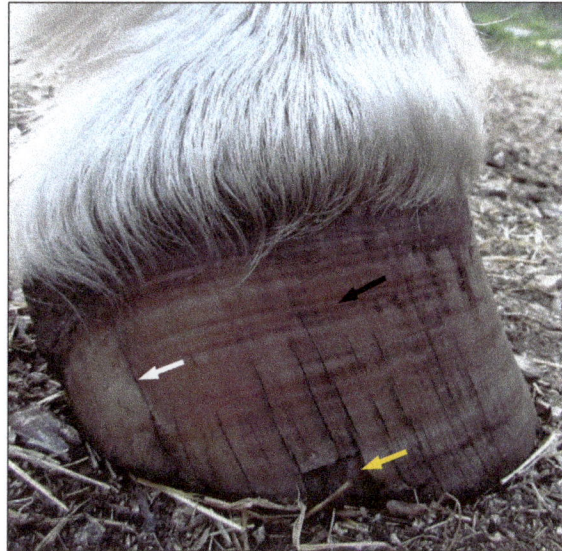

(Figure 2-2) *Black dashed arrows* trace a *mass accretion wave* while pointing to the leading edge of the wave. This wave commenced approximately .5 *hgc* (about four months) earlier — the day she arrived at our Paddock Paradise. The wave created a thicker, stronger, and more stable wall above the leading edge of the wave. *White arrow* points to feint remnant of quarter crack, also healed by the same wave. *Black solid arrow* points to remnant of stripped outer wall.

(Figure 2-3) 1 *hgc* (about nine months) has transpired. The mass accretion wave has done its job, and there are no blemishes left in the hoof wall. Measurements reveal that the angle differential between the clubfoot and the left front hoof did not change. But in every other respect the clubfoot was as naturally shaped and sound as its left pair.

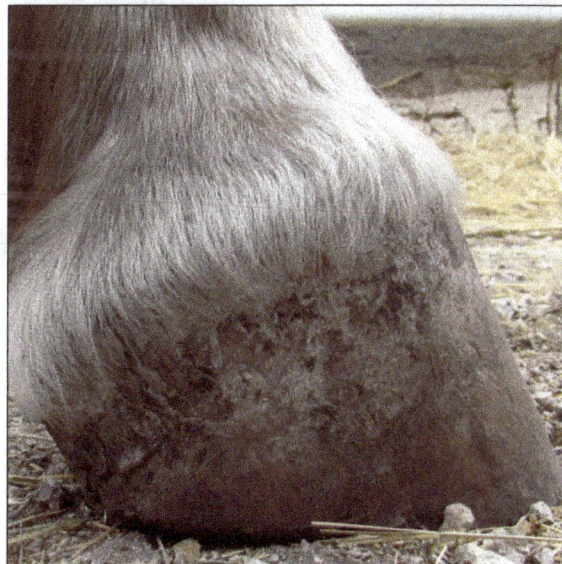

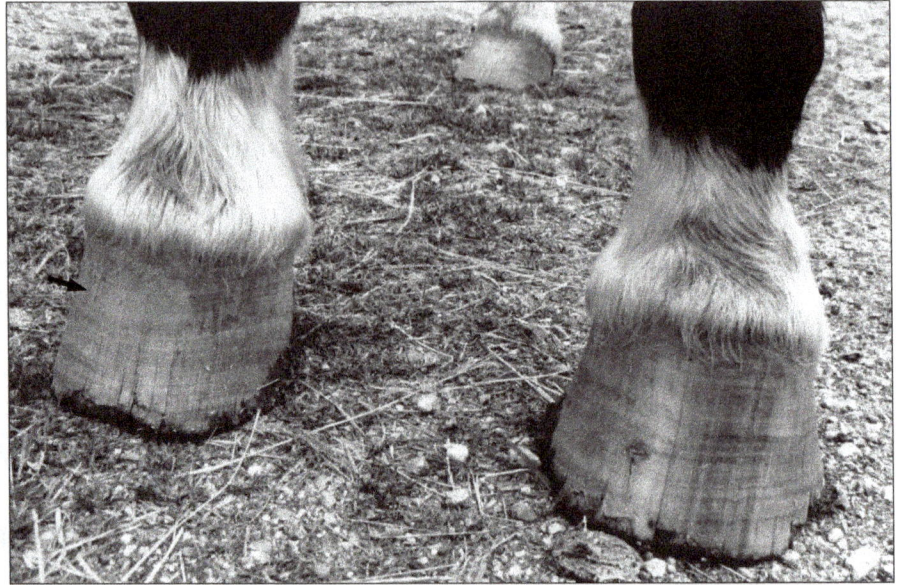

Audrey's hooves as they looked soon after she arrived at the AANHCP field headquarters in early March/2013. *Arrow* points to RF clubfoot. Life on track soon brought the Healing Field to bear, however, and we were able to witness the extraordinary healing powers of nature transform her hooves and body (*facing page*).

*hgc. The Natural Trim: Basic Guidelines. p. 43. 1 *hgc* is equivalent to about 9 months, the approximate time it takes to grow an entire new hoof.

After one *hoof growth cycle*, (*hgc**), life in Paddock Paradise and a reasonably natural diet restored her damaged hooves (*above*). However, measurements taken with the Hoof Meter Reader revealed that the right front hoof was significantly clubbed — but she did not falter at the trot. The toe angle of the clubbed foot exceeded its left front pair by 11 degrees of elevation.

Upon her arrival, I also began to search for the cause of her clubfoot. I palpated her lumbar spine and found many hard protrusions. But further inspection also revealed a deep dimpled scar that had formed on her left hip (*left* and Figure 2-4). It's not clear how this happened. The *double arrow* (Figure 2-4) suggests a strong diagonal relationship to the clubfoot, probably exacerbated by the spinal injury. I speculated that the two traumas — one chronic to her spine and the other acute to the hip muscle — converged during her early training, which would have brought that phase of her life to an abrupt end. Photos of her as a foal showed there was no evidence of a clubfoot, and I wonder if her previous caretakers had ever recognized it for what it was. Nevertheless, in spite of all her body issues, she integrated with the other four horses over the next week and, as we expected, took immediately to her new lifestyle on track without issue.

A decision had been made from the first day of her arrival to study the impact of Audrey's forthcoming life in Paddock Paradise on her hooves and across her body. From earlier experiences with navicular horses that were also laminitic, I knew how to resolve the influences of laminitis to confirm a clubbed hoof in conventional boarding operations. But what I did not know is whether these healing waves would impact the 11 degree angle differential between the two front

(**Figure 2-4**) *Double arrow* traces the diagonal relationship between Audrey's right front clubfoot and her left hind hip injury. However, significant protrusions along her lumbar spine suggested that riding her at an early age likely contributed to the clubfoot as well. I surmised that the two traumas may have coincided, thereby ending her "career" as a reining horse. Her previous caretakers subsequently used her as a brood mare before letting her go for easy trail or arena riding. The buckskin gelding behind her on track was her foal, reunited in our Paddock Paradise years later.

(**Figure 2-5**) Audrey's hooves eight months after entering our Paddock Paradise. *Arrow* points to leading edge of healing wave in RF hoof. A second, and final, wave emerged shortly after in both hooves. Although each hoof underwent changes in terms of overall mass that impacted their sizes, shapes, and growth angles, the 11 degree angle differential remained the same throughout her life in our Paddock Paradise.

hooves in our rugged Paddock Paradise track system. At the end of one *hgc*, Audrey was completely sound in all her gaits living 24/7 with four other horses on track. Although the toe angles for both front hooves did change over time due to natural hoof care and natural lifestyle changes, the 11 degree angle differential remained the same during her entire stay in our Paddock Paradise [Figures 2-5 and 2-6 (*next page*)]. This to me was incontrovertible evidence that the existence of a clubfoot does not necessarily cannote to lameness. But the fact that many horses are clubfooted and also lame (falter at the trot), simply means there are more factors to look at. I will sort through these in the concluding chapter of this book.

(*Overleaf*) Paddock Paradise as a healing field. pp. 18-23.

cont'd on page 24

Figure 2-6. Higher angle range is Audrey's RF clubfoot which quickly settled at approximately 64 degrees. Though high, it lies within the natural angle ranges I sampled in my wild horse studies. Lower angle range is for her LF hoof which, at 53-54 degrees, hovered very close to the median/average value for wild horse front hooves. I calculated a permanent angle differential of 11 degrees as a close approximation based on this data.

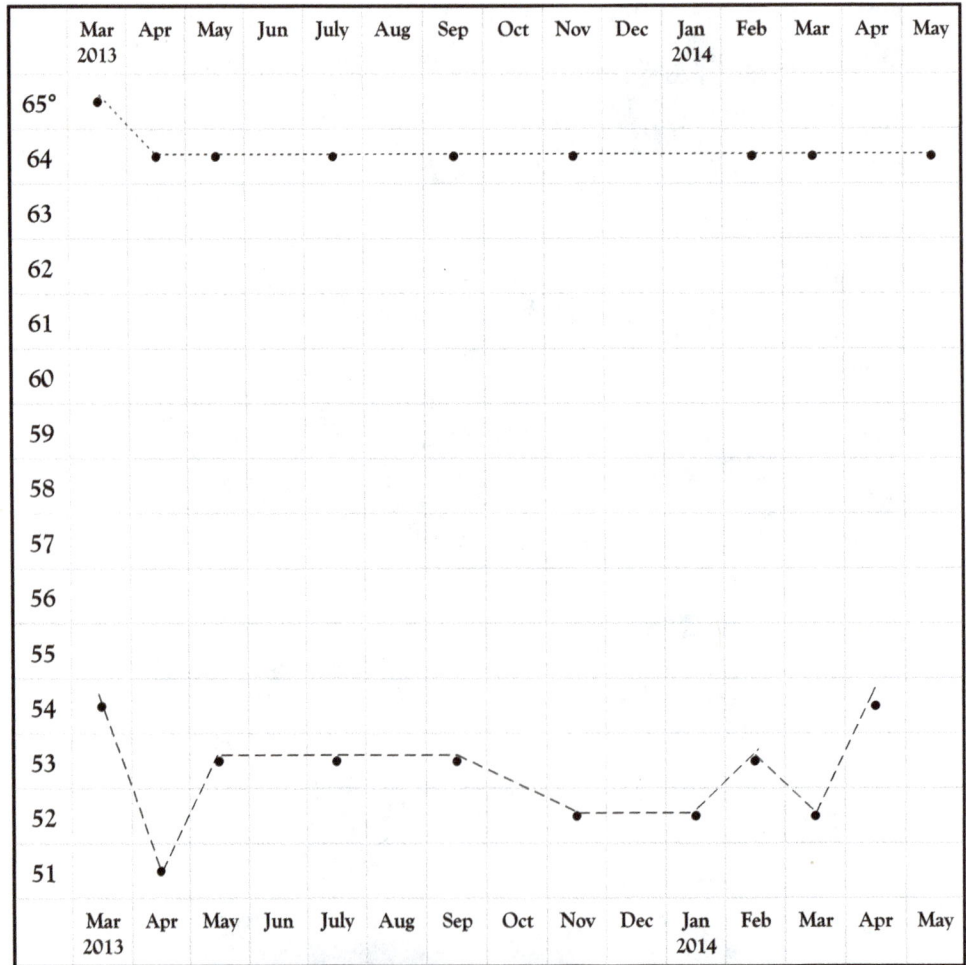

Our horses commonly pulled hay out from the netted bags to eat off the ground. Audrey has no problem using the LF clubfoot for this ground level "foraging."

Audrey trots over her RF club-foot without faltering, which was the case in all her gaits..

(*Left*) **Audrey** is in the front, once more using **her very stable** RF clubfoot to negotiate our track. The horses seem indecisive about staying below, or heading up the steep incline in the background to the upper track. (*Below*) A "decision" is made and suddenly all take flight to the ridge top.

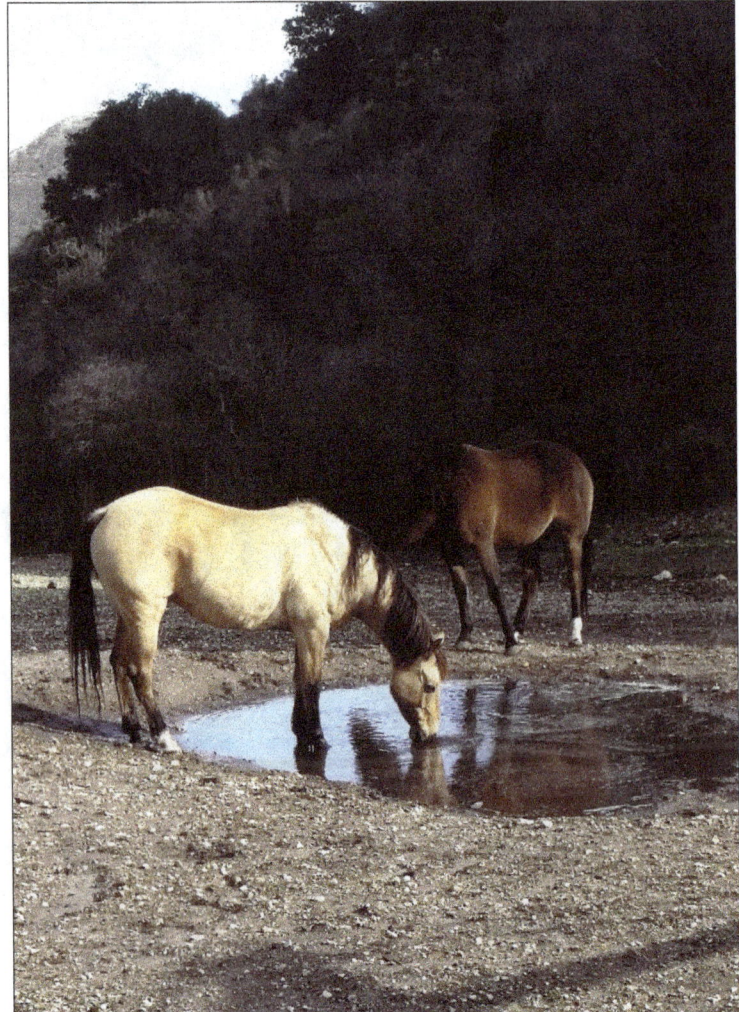

(Top) In Paddock Paradise, horses eat together as they do in the wild. Such socialization (dietary behavior) is another important "lesson from the wild."

(Above) The horse's ability to bend and flex facilitates natural movments and also natural hoof care. What we call "sequencing" — how we move around the horse during trimming — is based on the horse's natural gaits as they are athletically developed in Paddock Paradise. It is a fact that "straight" horses living in Paddock Paradise are significantly easier to trim than conventionally boarded horses.

(Right) Drinking water from "water holes" is the most natural and healthful way for horses. It is what happens in the wild. Nature has designed the hooves to stand in water and in mud while the horse drinks. The digestive biology of the horse is adapted to such behavior, and is highly recommended in the planning of any Paddock Paradise.

One of our "beta" geldings is digging for roots to eat we didn't even know existed. Horses naturally use their hooves as "tools," yet another important "lesson from the wild."

Formations based on pecking order ("relative dominance") characterized our band's movements in our Paddock Paradise tracking system. Audrey is at the rear on the left. *White arrow* points to damaged area of her left hip.

Audrey stands over the younger horses while they sleep. Sand was trucked in to provide the horses with a "rolling area." In the wild, family bands converge at such sites, each band taking its turn based on relative dominance. Similar behavior occurs at watering holes.

cont'd from page 17

The significance and import of Paddock Paradise to Audrey's healing cannot be ignored. We also found that the protrusions along her lumbar spine dissipated along with the stress rings in her hoof walls. The stress rings abated because of her new diet, discussed in the next chapter. But the spinal healing required other healing forces. Hence, the relationship of navicular trauma in the lumbar vertebrae to crookedness and extreme horsemanship practices was an important focus in accounting for the healthful changes in Audrey's back.

Double Back

Coming to mind at the time was what Xenophon called the "double-back," a characteristic the ancient Greek General attributed to a strong back capable of carrying a rider.* Saddles had not yet been developed beyond simple pads, and the double-back no doubt served to protect the spine recessed below the adjacent longitudinal muscles. I had witnessed such backs among Great Basin wild horses, conspiculously so in the monarch (breeding) stallions (*below*). All of the horses in our Paddock Paradise had also developed double-backs (Figure 2-7 and 2-8). This seemed consistent with Xenophon's observations and my own in wild horse country.

*"A double-back is easier to sit upon and stronger." Xenophon. *Art of Horsemanship*. p. 17.

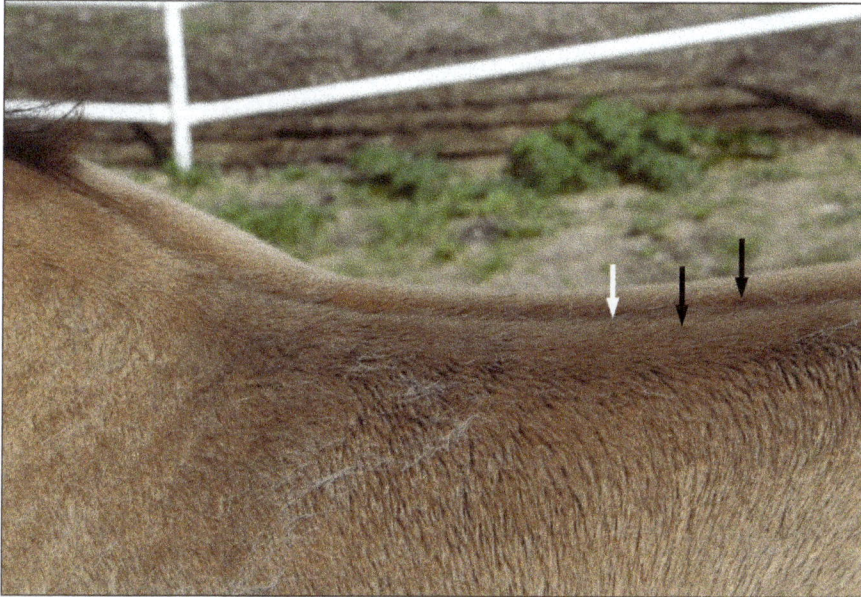

(Figure 2-7) All of our horses had "double backs," a term coined by Xenophon 2500 years ago to described the muscles of the horse's back. They were a consequence of their lifestyles in our Paddock Paradise, since none of the horses were ridden or trained there. The muscles of the double back parallel segments of the thoracic, lumbar, and pelvic vertebrae. But it is the region of the lumbar spine where navicular due to extreme riding practices is most likely to happen. *White arrow* points to recessed spine; *black arrows* point to the two ridges of the double-back; these are muscles critical to natural collection described by Podhajsky. Riding horses without double-backs is nother pathway to navicular.

(Figure 2-8) Xenophon was principally concerned with the thoracic vertebrae, as this is where his soldiers would sit. But, technically, the double-back continues further back along the spine to both the lumbar and pelvic vertebrae. (*Left*) *White arrow* points to recessed pelvic spine; *black arrows* point to the two muscular ridges of the double-back. (*Below*) Armed with her double-back and RF clubfoot, Audrey gallops in the rain up the steep hill of our track. Hard to believe this is the same animal that arrived at our Paddock Paradise a year earlier in a frightful condition.

In the wild, newborn are soon up and moving with the family band, whose survival demands that young and old alike get to where the "lead mare" takes them to for water, forage, and even "meet ups" with other bands roaming in or near their well-defined home range. The rugged environment challenges the foal's vitality, building powerful muscles, double-backs, and hooves as tough as the rocks they must negotiate in their daily travels.

Thinking of Podhajsky's methods of straightening horses such that they are able to bend naturally into a turn and also engage the powerful joints of the hindquarters in either lead to facilitate natural collection, I turned also once more to America's Great Basin wild horses. From birth, the wild horse must meet the many challenges of living in the arid, rugged Great Basin (*above*). Crookedness in the womb is, as a consequence, naturally uncoiled by their vigorous lifestyles — apparent to anyone who has witnessed them in their home ranges. The foal is up and moving within minutes following birth, soon tagging along at their mother's side as part of the family band, which is perpetually on the move to find water and food, and "meet ups" with other family and bachelor bands. The threat of predators also contributes to the horse's vitality, such as their natural enemy in wild horse country — the mountain lion — who feeds upon the wild horse young.* But whether physically present or not, predation lives within their psyche.

*"Influence of Predation by Mountain Lions on Numbers and Survivorship of a Feral Horse Population." John W. Turner, Jr. and Michael L. Morrison *The Southwestern Naturalist*, Vol. 46, No. 2 (Jun., 2001), pp. 183-190 (8 pages) Published By: Southwestern Association of Naturalists.

Many other lifestyle forces straighten the horse's body in the wild. I have identified many in two of my books, *The Natural Horse: Lessons From the Wild*, and *Paddock Paradise: A Guide to Natural Horse Boarding*. In fact, *Paddock Paradise* was written to encourage horse owners to adapt the "lessons from the wild" to infuse their own horses with the same wilderness vitality in the Paddock Paradise habitat. Such was the case in our own Paddock Paradise where the horses engaged in many, if not most, of the behaviors seen among wild horses. The ability to be straight came as naturally to our horses as those living in the wild, witnessed in the behaviors of our horses.

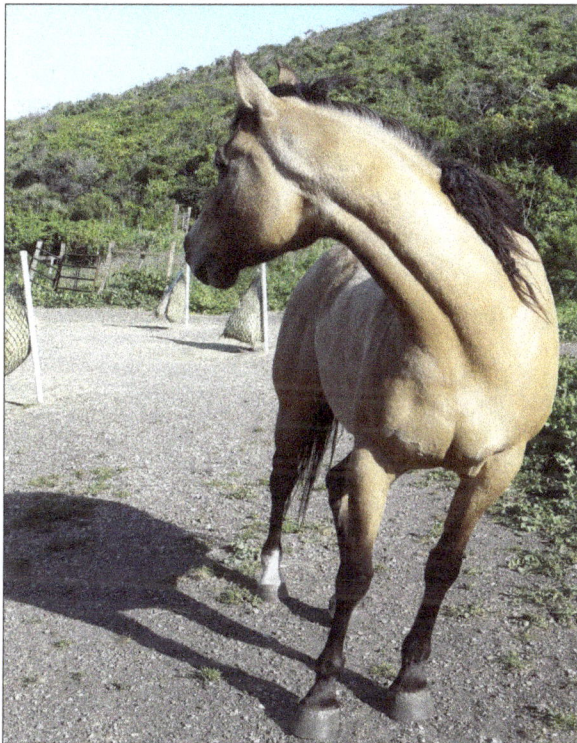

Bending in any direction is a natural consequence of life in Paddock Paradise, as it is in the horse's wild state. Powerful neck muscles, able to bend or flex, coupled to strong double-backs, and muscular hindquarters, all facilitate natural locomotive behavior — nature's defense against navicular.

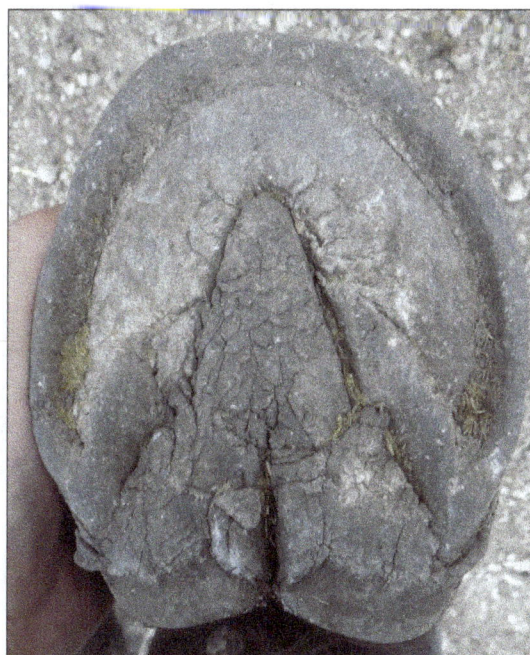

Another consequence of being "straight" and moving naturally in Paddock Paradise, are the hooves which are rendered tough as the rocks they move over effortlessly without blemish nor hypersensitivity. But there are certain challenges in trimming such hooves shaped in a Paddock Paradise that closely simulates the Great Basin as ours was. These are explained in my book, *The Natural Trim: Basic Guidelines* (2019).

NHC Pillar #2
A Reasonably Natural Diet

I mentioned in the Introduction the importance of diet in dealing with navicular. Of the hundreds of navicular horses I have faced over the years, I can't recall a single case where the horse wasn't also suffering from either acute or chronic laminitis. While I do not believe that whatever caused navicular also caused laminitis, except the person riding and feeding the horse, the two are linked by common horse care practices shared by horse owners all around the planet. The dietary link is fostered by the feed industry, which continues to create horse feeds that cause laminitis, and the practice of putting horses in pastures that also cause laminitis. The riding practices that lead to navicular were discussed in Chapter 1, although I will add more to that discussion in the next chapter. But in both cases, industry and horse owner, it is the biology of the horse that is clearly not understood. If it were, navicular and laminitis would be as scarce in domestication as they are in wild horse country. Which is to say, non-existent. But since that isn't the case, the immediate task is to distinguish the signs and symptoms of both, and then go after their respective causes. This is necessary because a horse that is in pain due to laminitis and whose hooves are deformed by laminitis, can interfere with an unfettered diagnosis of navicular.

NHC science has elucidated laminitis causality and a remedy through changes in diet. Verifiable signs and symptoms of laminitis are included in Table 3-1. Anyone who's had a horse that is laminitic should be able recognize many of these. Note the transition from sub-clinical (no pain) to clinical (pain) to chronic. Chronic laminitis deforms the hoof, often catastrophically so, and, not infrequently, causes the horse's death. My opinion is that many horses dying from chronic laminitis are also navicular without the owner even recognizing it.

(Continued on page 28)

Table 3-1
Three Stages of Laminitis
and Their Signs and Symptoms*

Any number of possible triggers

↓

Sub-clinical Stage

↙   ↓   ↘

Widening of laminae	Stress rings in outer wall	Blood in laminae

↓

Clinical (Acute) Stage

Any Sub-clinical or Clinical Signs and Symptoms, plus any of the following:

↙   ↓   ↘

Foot pain	Tendency to stand and lie down repeatedly	Heavy breathing
Founder stance	Constant left-right, right-left shifting of body weight	Sweating
Pounding pulse (foot)	Shock-Death	Anxiety

↓

Chronic Stage

Any Sub-clinical or Clinical Signs and Symptoms, plus any of the following:

↙   ↓   ↘

Cresty neck	Hoof slough	Off-on lameness
Severe hoof deformity	Lamellar wedge	Thrush
Minor hoof deformity	P3-rotation	Unnatural hair growth
Dropped sole	P3-penetration	Colic

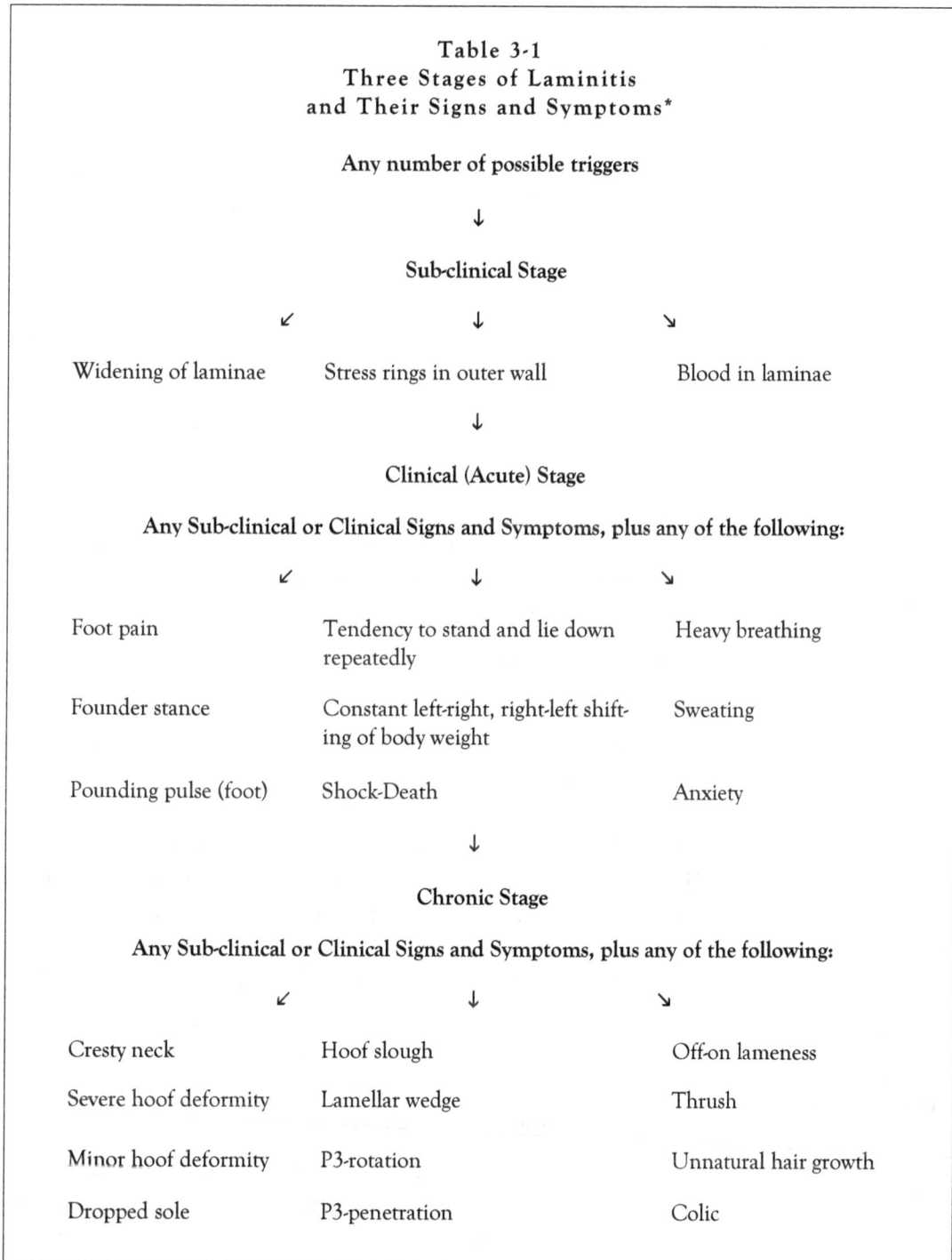

*Reference: Jaime Jackson. *Laminitis: A Plague of Unconscionable Proportions – Healing and Protecting Your Horse Using Natural Principles and Practices* (2016), Table 4-1, p. 25.

Table 3-2 Natural and Artificial Laminitis Triggers* (*Triggers may vary by quantity, concentration, and frequency.)			
Naturally occurring	**Artificial ("intentional human manufactured")**		
Vegetative	**Biological**	**Chemical**	**Agricultural**
Grasses, legume plants, and other vegetation that manufacture sugars.	• Vaccinations • Antibiotics • Steroids	• Fertilizers • Herbicides • Parasiticides • Pergolide • NSAIDS • Glyphosate • Propionic acid	All free sugars: cane, molasses, beet pulp, fructose, and artificial sweeteners.
			Feeds containing free sugars; corn, barley; waste products such as wheat middlings, mineral oil, rice bran, and formaldehyde; and anti-fungal chemicals such as propionic acid.

Table 3-2 summarizes "triggers" of laminitis — the most common things that are fed or put into horses that cause the laminitic inflammation. Much of laminitis can be prevented if horse owners take these triggers seriously.

Laminitis causality

Laminitis begins not in the foot, or hoof, but in the horse's intestines as a result of diet and other things put into the horse. Thus, the inflammatory response of laminitis within the foot is an indirect one. What happens is that these things that are toxic to all horses act upon the diverse colonies of bacteria living there together in symbiosis. Conditions in the horse's hind gut turn acidic, favoring the proliferation of some of the worst types of these microbes,* while killing off others not believed to be harmful. Laminitis researchers have found these harmful bacteria in the horse's foot, traveling through the vascular system to get there. While they also get to other places in the horse's body and cause damage there too, I'm limiting this discussion to what they do to the foot.

Having reached the growth coriums of the foot, their mere presence impacts the enzymes responsible for disengaging the bridge securing the inner hoof wall to the lowermost bone of the foot, so that the hoof may grow down and past the bone. These enzymes are incited to proliferate out of control, breaking down the bridge attachments faster than the growth coriums can repair them.** This painful breakdown is what is called laminitis; thus, it is a symptom of the bigger problem beginning back in the horse's digestive system. Because the pain-

Streptococcus bovis and *Streptococcus equinus* have been identified by Pollitt and others as offending bacteria. Christopher C. Pollitt. *Equine Laminitis – Current Concepts* (May 2008: Rural Industries Research and Development Corporation, Australian Government). RIRDC Publication No 08/062. RIRDC UQ-118A. Section 4-9, p. 23.

**Pollitt. *Equine Laminitis – Current Concepts.* Section 3-7, p. 17.

ful and devastating impact of these toxins and microbes can occur across the entire horse's body, I've given it a name: Whole Horse Inflammatory Disease ("WHID").

NHC science and practices go after the cause of laminitis, in other words, WHID, while treating symptoms such as foot pain with conventional veterinary medications to control inflammation and mitigate the horse's suffering; in some cases, we recommend standing the horse in ice water to inhibit enzyme proliferation. According to Laminitis researcher, Chris Pollitt:

> The precise, molecular pathogenesis of acute laminitis is unknown. The diverse effects of cryotherapy, however, have the potential to interrupt many of the pathophysiological mechanisms that are likely to occur during the developmental and acute phases of the disease.*

*Pollitt. *"Equine Laminitis – Current Concepts.* Section 10-2,3, p. 69-70.

WHID, however, is only resolved by detoxifying the horse. This is a two part process: One must cease feeding the toxic substances to the horse; at the same time, begin feeding the NHC recommended diet for horses.* The transition can be pretty complicated, and in the worst cases of laminitis, I help horses and their owners through the ISNHCP Veterinary Consultation Service.**

*Available at: https://www.aanhcp.net/products/aanhcp-recommended-diet

**www.ISNHCP.net

Once toxicity begins to abate, and the new diet takes over repopulating a healthy digestive system, pain due to laminitis will also diminish and the horse will begin to move more freely. At this point, critical natural hoof care begins. If the hooves were chronically deformed (very common, and sometimes horrifically so), then more time will be needed for additional *hgcs* to generate more healthy growth (healing mass accretion waves) and more natural movement. Somewhere along the way, with WHID now under control, the signs and symptoms attributable to navicular will begin to reveal themselves. A diagnosis can then be confirmed and a pathway to healing laid. The final two pillars will be critical to this objective.

Natural Horsemanship

Natural horsemanship (NHC Pillar #3) is defined as the horse moving willfully within the specie's natural gait complex. This complex of movements includes those natural gaits and variations seen among America's wild, free-roaming horses living in the U.S. Great Basin: 4-beat walk, 2-beat trot, and 3-beat canter.* Such natural movement is rooted in the behavioral biology of the species, as seen in the wild. Extreme violations of the specie's natural gait complex by riders invariably result in navicular. So, the problem isn't just about bad riding methods, but about the rider's ignorance of, or indifference to, the horse's behavioral biology. In fact, I believe this disconnect between "natural movement" and "natural behavior" by equestrians may lie at the core of navicular breakdown in horses.**

There is more than one way to look at the foundations for natural horsemanship based on the wild horse model. One is through the natural gaits, which I use to help me diagnose and predict navicular (Chapter 6). The other is through common sense, which I relied on during my formative years as a natural rider. I'll share some of that here as such thinking kept my horses "navicular free." I will add that I never had riding lessons from anyone — my horses have always been my teachers.

- If it takes shoeing a horse to get them to do something, then we are probably wise not to make them do that at all.

- We shouldn't try to teach a horse their natural gaits — how to walk, trot, and canter — because they already know how from birth. This also includes each gait's variations: stride extensions and contractions ("passage" and "piaffe"), turns on the hindquarters and forehand, "airs above the ground," and so forth.* All we're going to do is confuse and screw things up for them. Just let them show us how, and they will do it willingly on their own if necessity says so in their own minds. Many equestrian disciplines are full of navicular because these equine theatrics have become objectives, forcing horses to comply. Compliance invariably means deploying "warfare riding equipment," discussed shortly .

*The 4-beat gallop may be a corruption of the canter. The many other "gaits" we see in domestic horses appear also to be man-made corruptions of the horse's natural gaits, and may be causal to navicular along with riding, training, and breeding practices that induce them in horses.

***"Behavior and Movement of the Wild Horse." Jaime Jackson. *The Natural Horse: Lessons From the Wild.* pp. 31-66.

*But just like with humans, not all horses are predisposed or physically capable of doing all of what we think of as "advanced" movements. Paddock Paradise is very revealing of what individual horses are willfully capable of doing. Compelling horses to do otherwise is another door opener to navicular.

- Likewise, we shouldn't try to teach a horse how to "collect" themself, because they already know how to do that too — also from birth. Collection is a big term in equestrian sports, full of navicular too. So, let the horse collect themself as they see fit.

- Be happy with simple trail riding. Your horse will love you for that. They can walk, trot, canter and even do other things, all on their own! Learn how to ask them, and they'll do it gladly. But if they can't and won't, review the signs and symptoms for navicular and make sure that's not the problem. Ask yourself, is my horse "straight" or "crooked?"

- Another problem most horse owners will have to face up to at some point is that not every horse is going to like them as a riding partner for whatever reason. In fact, count on that. If, as an example, it's not your horsemanship skills that has led to a bittersweet relationship, then they may just not like you period as a person. It's time to find a horse who really likes you, and you really like them! Who wants to be in a relationship full of force, passive resistance and dread? In the wild, horses are picky as heck when it comes to who they want to be with. It's not a giant love festival out there! Equine friendships in the wild are based on mutual affection, meaning they want to be in the relationship. Because in the wild, any horse can run off to be with other horses of their choice. And that's what happens. There are no stalls, or paddocks, or fences, or people, to stop them. So, if your horse sees you coming and heads off in the opposite direction, or just doesn't want to be "caught," guess what? Consider looking for another equine partner!

- Use seat and leg aids to initiate a natural gait, to sustain it, to speed it up or slow it down, to change its direction, to stop it, or to change it to another gait. Learning to do this will require much practice and close attention to how the horse moves at liberty. But plan on spending as much or more time working with the horse to confirm the pressure of your body aids to the gait are understood. An example, the position of your pelvis and legs together should correspond to the back and legs of the horse in whatever gait you are moving. If you are "signaling" the horse to canter, you don't want to be sitting (pelvis and legs) in the position that corresponds to the trot! Further, if signaling for the canter, your pelvis and legs should be oriented to the horse's lead. In other words, if your body orientation is aligned to initiate the right lead, don't expect to go to the left! I will add here that if a horse cannot take a particular lead, and your body is correctly aligned to initiate that lead, the horse is probably crooked and vulnerable to navicular if not straightened.

- Use vocal commands (as necessary) to communicate with the horse as a way to reinforce the seat/leg commands. Horses do not speak or actually understand a word of what we are saying, but will get the gist of it through sound-to-pressure association. Remember, horses are sentient beings trying to figure us out too, like what it is we want from them. So clarity in establishing the basics of the aids is of supreme importance.

- Teach the vocal commands (e.g., to move forward or halt in a gait) from the ground with the horse in hand. These lessons will transfer naturally to the saddle. Praise and reward the horse for every inkling of cooperation. Horses appreciate these acts of kindness, and will give back through cooperation accordingly.

- Dispense with "warfare riding equipment" if you truly want a good relationship with your horse based on mutual trust and affection. This means getting rid of bits of any type, poll pressure headsets (e.g., "bitless bridles"), tie-downs, spurs and whips (*below*).* Half of

* (*Below*) I've added circles where the rider's attack zones are. These are not "aids," they are inhumane instruments of torture to force the horse into compliance.

Me during the late 70s. No whip, no spurs, no bit, just a sheepskin covered nose band on a bosal I made myself. A few of my cardinal rules of natural horsemanship:

- Choose a horse that clearly likes you, and you like them. Otherwise, change partners.
- Make sure your temperaments are a good match. Or there will be trouble!
- Never pull on the horse's mouth. You wouldn't like it done to you, and they don't like it either.
- Keep reins loose so the horse can set their neck and head for natural collection. It's not your job to hold or force their head in or into position. It's what they do!
- Use your seat and legs to command the horse's gait, speed, tempo, rhythm, and cadence.
- Teach the horse what you want them to do — don't expect them to read your mind! Talk to them about it in an encouraging voice and reward them for making the effort.
- Develop your own personal language (words) for vocal commands. Horses can learn these by association. Other riders may not understand it, but so what? They're not riding your horse.
- Command your horse — be the alpha, not a beta, or they will command you. It's their "way."
- Ride with other riders. But pay attention to pecking order! And don't ride with horse abusers.
- Understand "ear radar" — the horse is talking to you!
- No tie downs, martingales, whips, bits, or spurs.
- Use the lightest saddle possible that fits the horse's double-back and your butt and legs. Both of you need to feel comfortable, not just you.
- (*Below*) If you are out of shape, don't exercise, and are lazy, get yourself a 4-wheeler instead and reward your horse with a life in Paddock Paradise for putting up with you in the first place.

these contraptions are devised to control the horse's head and mouth, and restrain forward motion. The other are designed to drive the horse into the restraining devices. It's not that horses "accept" these devices, they really have no say in the matter. Try using a simple bosal with a padded sheepskin noseband with thin leather reins (*above*). So "disarmed," the meaning of natural horsemanship will surely come into clearer focus.

- Keep a loose rein. Seeking "lightness" rather than "force" is core to natural horsemanship. Invariably, force leads to "heaviness," resistance with the horse leaning heavily on the reins — enough to wear your arms down from exhaustion — or refusing contact altogether. Use the reins as "guides" — extensions of your arms and hands to reinforce the seat, leg, and vocal aids. Pulling back on the reins to stop a horse from going forward is a horse "out of control."

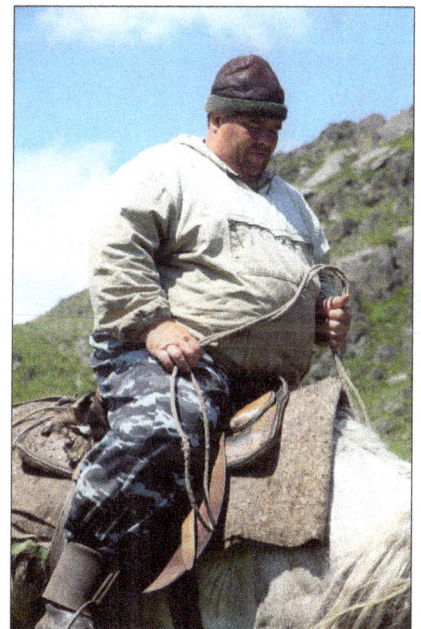

A horse will naturally slow down or stop altogether if rein tension corresponds to seat, leg, and vocal aids. There are some natural riders so adept at being in harmony with their horses that they've dispensed with the reins altogether.

- Don't confuse "praise" and "reward" with "bribery." They are not the same. Bribery inures to greediness, impatience, intolerance, and even meanness in horses, as in "biting the hand that feeds you" — and that's how we know we're engaging in bribery! Save yourself.

- Forsake teaching "gimmickry." Horses are not stupid and they're probably not amused by such things. Anymore than "stall toys." They simply put up with it and can't wait until it's over with. Natural riders consider such antics as "circus."

- If you are going to ride your horse anymore than easy trail riding (also called "free forward riding"), then the issue of "straightness" (discussed earlier) is on the table for serious discussion and action. If a horse isn't straight, then they can't naturally collect themselves, and the door to navicular is wide open. If you don't know how this is done, then you are going to have to find someone who does and is willing to teach you. This can get tricky. But you are now armed with information that will help you find such a knowledgeable person. First, you should check out their own horse or horses. You will need to use the Hoof Meter Reader (4th Pillar) and look for the classic signs of navicular and pre-navicular — and also chronic laminitis. If they are there, and the trainer has no awareness of why in the NHC sense of understanding, I would look elsewhere. And if they are known for riding young horses, once more look elsewhere. Finally, if they are using spurs, whips, bits or pressure headsets, and tie downs, and their horses are shod, still keep looking. Instead, ask about for someone who's known to be a "good rider" but that few have heard of elsewhere. Chances are they are our genuine natural riders who have figured it all out, usually on their own or from someone who taught them and was a natural rider themself. If you see them ride, or compete, they are the ones who aren't pulling on the horse's mouth, using force to drive them forward (e.g. "onto the bit"), and the horse is simply doing what has been asked of them because they want to please and because their owner is kind to them. They will also be navicular free. But, chances are good that your horse will be naturally and athletically "straight" if they're living in a rugged Paddock Paradise, especially if they were born and grew up in one. If you have such a horse, pay attention to them closely. They will be a better teacher than the most famous trainer in the world.

- When you head out on the trail, or wherever you're riding, bring along a riding partner/s. Horses are prey herd animals and need other horses to feel secure. It is the rare alpha horse who goes willingly alone, or the rarer beta horse who trusts their owner/rider enough to also go it alone and not be trying to head back to the barn. Better to ride with other horse owners whom you respect. But beware of potential alpha-beta conflicts among horses riding together, as pecking order will need to be facilitated to avoid aggression between horses with human casualties "in between."

- Take a clinic with an ISNHCP clinician and learn to "sequence" your horse. Sequencing, as it is defined in the ISNHCP Natural Trim Training Program, is a way to communicate with horses using the natural gait complex, praise and reward, and relative dominance ("RD"). Its application, however, goes far beyond trimming horses. In fact, it is a specialized form of ground training for both horse and human to help both better understand each other.

The Natural Trim

The 4th Pillar takes us into some of the nuances of the natural trim as they apply to navicular hooves. Data from the wild horse model is revealing of specific relationships between front left and right hooves: they are mirror images of each other, including size, proportion and angle of growth. But peculiar to the front hooves of the navicular horse is clubfootedness, with striking differences with respect to size and angle of growth, which I've discussed in earlier chapters. I also expressed my belief that the clubfoot is a specialized adaptation because there is no clinical evidence that its morphology is pathological.

I have measured hooves transforming into clubfeet and others clubbed before my arrival as the owner's NHC practitioner. I have yet to measure a clubfoot whose angle of growth gauged higher than what falls within the natural ranges for the species, that is, more than 65°. This is the opposite of chronically laminitic hooves whose growth angles may measure into negative (low angle) ranges, far off the natural angle ranges readable on the Hoof Meter Reader (HMR).

Left and right front hooves, where one is clubbed, will differ in toe angle by 3 to 10 or more degrees. My opinion is that the greater the angle differential, the more severe was the original trauma to the horse. This trauma could have occurred in a single catastrophic event, or from repeat events at the same body site or sites. The latter would suggest the animal was drugged to mitigate or conceal pain until it eventually became ineffective at concealing symptoms. Euthanasia typically follows. Surgical intrusion of the navicular zone would, as I've also discussed earlier in this book, simply induce navicular or compound the existing angle differential. In fact, surgical intrusions I have come across have left the horse completely lame (faltering), permanently so. And I have seen invasive trimming by both barefooters and farriers (and also vets) that attempted to cut out the natural clubbed heel conformation to force the growth angle down. This always fails, however, because the steeper angle of growth of the clubfoot does not occur there, but everywhere forward of the heels. Which is to say that heel

Figure 5-1

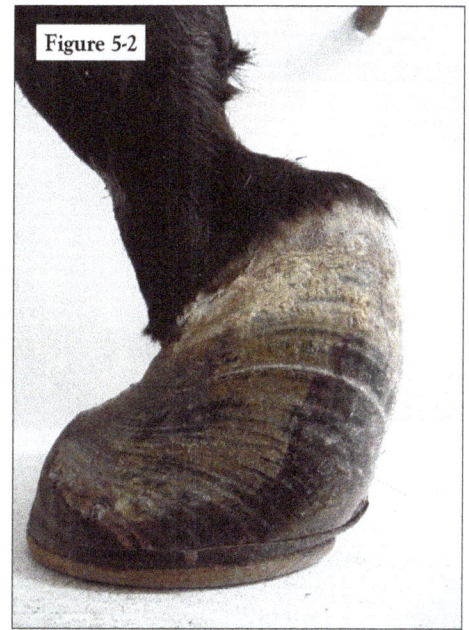

Figure 5-2

length is not causal to genuine clubfoot. In fact, heel length in the naturally trimmed clubfoot is no different than heel length in any other naturally shaped hoof given a genuine natural trim. Moreover, and this will no doubt astonish those who approach the clubfoot as pathological, *the clubfoot trims no different than any other naturally shaped hoof.*

If there is a complication ascertaining a clubfoot in a horse, it is the horse suffering from chronic laminitis with extreme "slipper toe" deformity and painful inflammation of the hooves' growth coriums. Figures 5-1 and 5-2* exemplify such laminitic hooves. In these cases, healing must begin with the 2nd Pillar (diet), meaning the horse must be detoxed of laminitis triggers so that inflammation subsides and normal hoof growth can ensue. Otherwise, the natural trim is powerless to make a difference.

As the natural trim takes effect on the hooves, the clubfoot's distinct angle differential will begin to emerge above the slipper toe.* Final resolution comes from comparing the angles of the new growth for both front hooves. If there is an angle differential of 3 or more degrees, the steeper angled hoof is likely clubbed, as the wild horse model dictates that left and right hooves grow naturally at the same toe angle. The *Advanced Guidelines* of the natural trim will be necessary to rein in the slipper toe until waves of new growth render toe angles readable within the domain of natural angle ranges on the HMR. The *Basic Guidelines* complement the *Advanced Guidelines* during the finishing parts of the trim, and eventually take over all the trimming once the slipper toe is re-

*This is a cadaver that was processed through one of my training clinics. It had been shod with pads at the time the horse was euthanized.

*However, if inflammation and pain have ended, my one case study suggests that angle differentials measured below the new growth on the slippered toe walls may also provide positive indicators of clubfootedness. More research is needed here. But if my initial findings are accurate then we can predict clubfoot, and, therefore, navicular, before slipper toe is resolved. See: Introduction. *The Natural Trim: Advanced Guidelines.* Jaime Jackson

The Natural Trim: Basic Guidelines. Jaime Jackson. (2019). *The Natural Trim: Advanced Guidelines.* Jaime Jackson. (2019).

solved.*

In conclusion, I will add that whatever the timeline nature dictates to confirm navicular through new growth in the slipper-toed hoof, the prognosis for soundness, in my opinion, is excellent when all 4 Pillars of NHC are acted upon in good faith. But with these caveats: Body damage has not resolved in permanent faltering with chronic pain; the "navicular zone" of the emerged clubfoot has not been subjected to surgery; and the heels have not been carved out by invasive trimming.

CHAPTER SIX
Examining Your Horse For Navicular

The tests for confirming navicular are surprisingly simple. There are four tests to complete. If, after reading my instructions below, you don't think you are up to the task, then I recommend that you obtain assistance from an ISNHCP NHC Practitioner,* or register for an online NHC veterinary consultation for support also through the ISNHCP.**

*www.AANHCP.net > Locate A Trimmer
**www.ISNHCP.net > NHC Veterinary Consultation Services

1. Check the horse's upper body for trauma.

So what you do here is review Chapter 1. Focus on the main areas of the spine and legs where navicular-related breakdown most commonly occurs. But note also in the discussion there that muscle and tendon damage may also be implicated. In any case, look for the tell-tale signs of navicular I've identified.

2. Examine the hooves.

Use the Hoof Meter Reader (HMR) to measure the toe angles of both front feet. Use my free online instructions for obtaining these measurements; you can also purchase a HMR at this link if you don't have one.* As explained, if there is an angle differential of 3 or more degrees, clubfoot is likely. But, here, you must be certain that your horse has been given a genuine natural trim; if in doubt, once more contact an ISNHCP practitioner at the link above for assistance. If your horse has been diagnosed with laminitis, then go to the 3rd test below.

*www.jaimejackson.com > Hoof Care > Measuring/Balancing Tools > Hoof Meter Reader for Horse Owners

3. Rule out hoof deformity and pain due to laminitis.

Hoof deformity and pain due to laminitis compromise a diagnosis of navicular. This was explained in Chapter 3. If your horse is laminitic, then you should register for the ISNHCP NHC Veterinary Consultation Service referenced above. Treating active laminitis is a higher priority than navicular because laminitis can be life-threatening. NHC defines laminitis as a medical emergency requiring veterinary intervention. If your horse is not diagnosed with laminitis, then move to the 4th test for navicular.

4. Lunge test for straightness and crookedness.

This test is used to confirm straightness or crookedness in

39

the horse, and if there is faltering at the trot. This test won't work for horses that are positive for laminitis as explained above in the 3rd test for navicular.

It is easier to conduct this test in a large open flat area with two persons: One person holding the lunge line at center, pivoting in place as the horse goes around in a circle; the other person driving the horse forward. A round pen will also work, providing its diameter is large enough (50 ft/15.24 m), and the lunge line is 25 ft./7.62 m long (Figure 6-1). In either location, the horse is driven at the trot — and only the trot — in both directions (that is, in both of the horse's leads). Three or four times around on each lead at the trot will be enough to complete the test.

The person holding the lunge line has several determinations to make: Does the horse falter? And on which lead? Is the lunge line slack or tight when going to the left, versus going to the right? *Slack* means the horse tends to fall in towards the center of the circle, resulting in a slack (loose) line.* This is tantamount to the horse "not taking the rein," as explained by Podhajsky in Chapter 1. *Tight* is the opposite, meaning the horse pulls away from the center, resulting in a lunge line that is tight (pulling away from you), the "stiff side" in the words of Podhajsky. If, for example, a horse "falls in" with a slack line on the left lead, they will pull away with a tight line when taking the right lead. In either case, the horse is said to be "crooked." A straight horse, in contrast, will move in either lead with the lunge line being neither slack nor tight.

This concludes the 4th test for navicular.

Sorting through your test results.

First, recognize that a reliable determination for navicular can't be made if the horse is actively suffering from pain due to laminitis and/or the hooves are deformed by chronic laminitis. You will require the professional services of an NHC Practitioner to help you end the horse's inflammatory state and restore the hooves to the natural ranges on the HMR. Once the laminitis is resolved, you can conduct the other tests for navicular with a high degree of certainty.

Continuing, measure toe angles for both front hooves using the HMR. If there is a significant angle differential of 3 or more degrees, clubfoot is probable. But this means the hooves have also been trimmed according to NHC guidelines for the natural trim. If you are not sure that they have been trimmed

*This presumes the person holding the line understands how to lunge a horse. A horse may decide to "go slack or tight" simply because they don't understand the lunge command being given — because the person on the other end of the line doesn't either. Not good! Advisable to find someone who can put a horse on a circle, or move to a round pen as explained above.

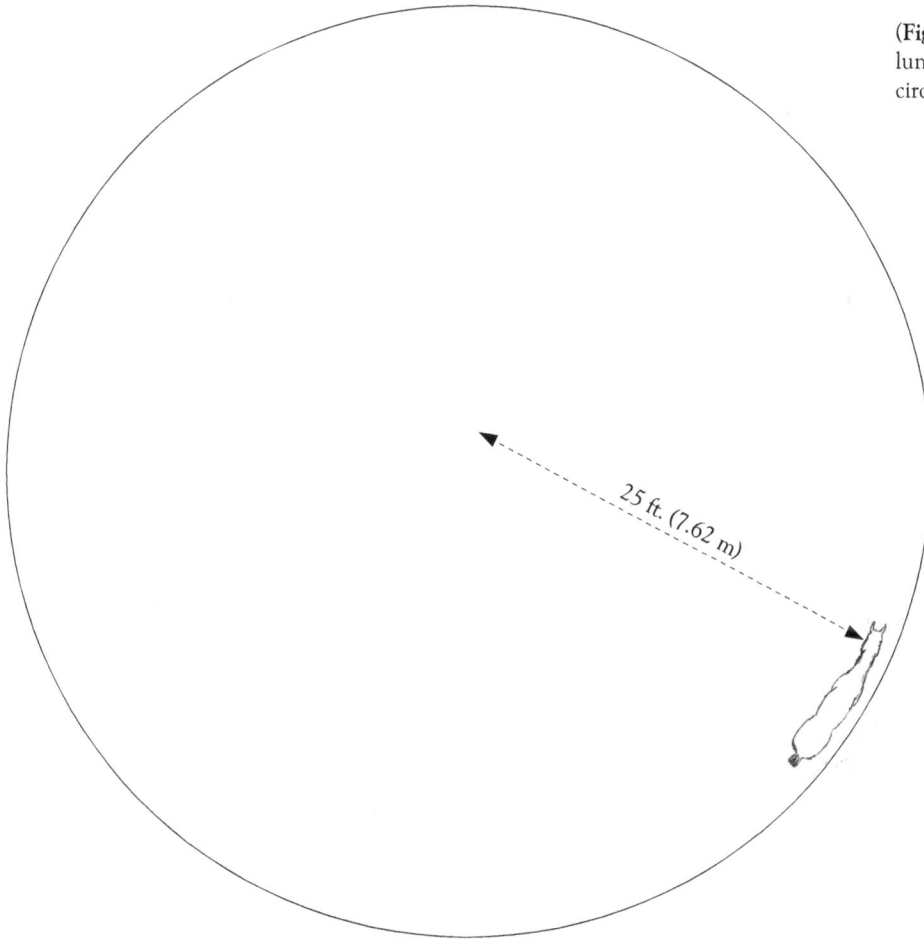

(**Figure 6-1**) *4th test for navicular.* Horse is lunged at the trot in both directions on a circle with a radius of 25 ft. (7.62 m).

25 ft. (7.62 m)

correctly, consult with an ISNHCP practitioner.*

Next, check the horse's upper body (anywhere above the hooves) for damage. If you have confirmed a clubfoot, damage will be either along the lumbar spine, or diagonally across from the clubfoot to the hind limb of the horse. For example, if the right front hoof is clubbed, then look to the lumber spine and then to the left hind limb. Damage is likely to have occurred at one or both of these locations on the diagonal. If severe damage to the horse occurred over one of the front hooves, then there may or may not be additional damage diagonally across to the lumbar spine and hind limb — but confirm anyways. The horse will likely falter at the trot. All of this is detective work to confirm a navicular diagnosis.

Finally, correlate your findings from the lunge test to the above. If the horse is faltering on one lead, you will find a corresponding clubfoot with damage to the upper body. Now, it may be that there is more than one location of severe body

*Or consider getting yourself trained to do this work. Most NHC practitioners are women with no previous training in hoof care. Go to: www.ISNHCP.net

damage to the horse, which I have seen more than once. In this case, the area of greater damage will determine which front hoof will club relative to the spine, and/or a specific diagonal correspondence to a hind limb. Your data gathered from all the tests will help you make this determination.

Concluding Thoughts

One may ask, if a horse has a measurable clubfoot determined with the HMR and observable upper body damage, does it mean that they will also falter at the trot, and, thus, be permanently lame? The answer is a guarded *maybe* and will depend on different factors.

Expect irreversible damage and lameness if there has been surgery conducted within the navicular zone, or the horse has suffered a devastating injury to the body from an accident in an unsafe environment tantamount to the example given in Chapter 1. Beyond these, *there is hope.* In Chapter 2, I explained what happened to the mare Audrey at the AANHCP Paddock Paradise in Lompoc, California. She had been chronically laminitic when she arrived, but which was completely healed within a single hoof growth cycle (1 *hgc*). Hardened lumps along her lumber spine dissipated completely as her double back developed from life on track 24/7. Her right front clubfoot, however, never resolved, sustaining a 11 degree angle differential relative to her left front hoof. Yet, she never faltered at the trot and moved vigorously in all her natural gaits. And this over rough, rocky ground in a one mile long track that was anything but flat, rising 600 feet from one end to the other. *But she was never ridden either.* Since our objective was soundness and vitality at liberty, and not putting someone on her back again, the answer to the leading question above is a firm negative — meaning, a healing is very viable, even likely. But outside a Paddock Paradise tracking system, the answer is one of uncertainty. For this reason, there is hope — and even certainty based on Audrey — that Paddock Paradise is the best environment we can put a navicular horse in to heal.

Jaime Jackson

Photo Credits

Cover (front)
- Jill Willis

Cover (back)
- *Top/left*: Copyright: <a href='https://www.123rf.com/profile_decade3d'>decade3d</a>
- *Top/right*: Jill Willis
- *Lower*: Jaime Jackson archives

Title page
- Jill Willis

P. 1
- *Facing page*: Jill Willis

P. 5
- Fig. 1-3: Kmusser CC (https://en.wikipedia.org/wiki/Great_Basin#/media/File:Greatbasinmap.png)

P. 9
- Jaime Jackson

P. 10
- http://www.a-laddin.com

P. 11
- Fig. 1-4: Jaime Jackson. *The Natural Horse: Lessons From the Wild*. p. 71.
- Fig. 1-5: Copyright: <a href='https://www.123rf.com/profile_anartelman'>Anar Babayev</a>

P. 13
- Fig. 1-6: Copyright: <a href='https://www.123rf.com/profile_decade3d'>decade3d</a>
- Fig. 1-7 (*left*): Jaime Jackson consultation archives.
- Fig. 1-7 (*right*): Vet Moves.com - Flickr: Bowed Tendons #2, CC BY 2.0, https://commons.wikimedia.org/w/index.php?curid=15999655

P. 14
- Jill Willis

P. 15-17
- All images: Jill Willis

P. 18
- Figure 2-6: Jaime Jackson
- Image below: Jill Willis

P. 19
- All images: Jill Willis

P. 20
- *Top/Above*: Jill Willis
- *Right*: Jaime Jackson

P. 21
- All images: Jill Willis

P. 22
- Jeff Foott

P. 23
- All images: Jill Willis

P. 24
- Neil Lockhart © www.123rf.com

P. 25
- All images: Jill Willis

P. 27
- Jaime Jackson. *Laminitis: A Plague of Unconscionable Proportions – Healing and Protecting Your Horse Using Natural Principles and Practices* (2016), Table 4-1, p. 25.

P. 28
- Jaime Jackson. *Laminitis: A Plague of Unconscionable Proportions – Healing and Protecting Your Horse Using Natural Principles and Practices* (2016), Table 3-1, p. 21.

P. 32
- Copyright: <a href='https://www.123rf.com/profile_vikarus'>Viktoria Makarova</a>

P. 33
- *Above*: Tommi Stevens (Jaime Jackson archives)
- *Below*: Copyright: <a href='https://www.123rf.com/profile_afhunta'>Aleksandr Frolov</a>

P. 37
- Fig. 5-1: Jill Willis
- Fig. 5-2: Jaime Jackson

P. 41
- Jaime Jackson

P. 47
- Jaime Jackson archives

Institute for the Study of
Natural Horse Care Practices
Founded 2009
www.ISNHCP.net
International Training Program
for Professional Natural Hoof Care Practitioners
ISNHCP Veterinary Consultation Services

Association for the Advancement of
Natural Horse Care Practices
Organization founded in 2000; 501c3 in 2004
WWW.AANHCP.NET
Advocacy organization for humane horse care practices
based on the U.S. Great Basin Wild, Free-Roaming Horse Model,
Listings of NHC Practitioners, NHC Bulletins and Articles

www.PaddockParadise.net
International website promoting natural boarding for horses
based on the concept of Paddock Paradise by Jaime Jackson

NHC Facebook and Instagram Sites
AANHCP, ISNHCP, Paddock Paradise, The Natural Trim

www.JaimeJackson.com
Author's website promoting NHC
Books, Tools/Equipment, Consultations

Equine Laminitis – Current Concepts. Christopher C. Pollitt. (May 2008: Rural Industries Research and Development Corporation, Australian Government). RIRDC Publication No 08/062. RIRDC UQ-118A.

Horseshoeing Theory and Hoof Care. Emery, Miller, and Van Hoosen. (1977, Lea & Febiger).

"Influence of Predation by Mountain Lions on Numbers and Survivorship of a Feral Horse Population." John W. Turner, Jr. and Michael L. Morrison. *The Southwestern Naturalist,* Vol. 46, No. 2 (Jun., 2001), pp. 183-190 (8 pages). Published By: Southwestern Association of Naturalists.

Laminitis: A Plague of Unconscionable Proportions. Jaime Jackson (2016).

Paddock Paradise: A Guide to Natural Horse Boarding. Jaime Jackson (1995, rev. 2018).

The Complete Training Of Horse and Rider. Alois Podhajsky (Doubleday/1966).

The Natural Horse: Lessons From the Wild. Jaime Jackson (1992, Northland Publishing; revised 2020).

The Natural Trim: Advanced Guidelines. Jaime Jackson (2019).

The Natural Trim: Basic Guidelines. Jaime Jackson (2019).

The Wild Horse's Foot. 2001 - 14th Annual Bluegrass Laminitis Symposium Notes. Written and presented January 2001 by R.F. (Ric) Redden, DVM.

Xenophon: The Art of Horsemanship. Translated by Morris H. Morgan (London: J. A. Allen & Co., 1962).

Zoo Paradise: A New Model for Humane Zoological Gardens. Jaime Jackson (2019).

www.ingramcontent.com/pod-product-compliance
Lightning Source LLC
Chambersburg PA
CBHW080630030426
42336CB00018B/3149